r and war's alarms.

Of War and War's Alarms

Of War and War's Alarms

Fiction and Politics in the Modern World

Paul J. Dolan

 THE FREE PRESS
A Division of Macmillan Publishing Co., Inc.
NEW YORK

Collier Macmillan Publishers
LONDON

The Free Press
A Division of Macmillan Publishing Co., Inc.
866 Third Avenue, New York, N.Y. 10022

Collier Macmillan Canada, Ltd.

Library of Congress Catalog Card Number: 75–11287

Printed in the United States of America

printing number

1   2   3   4   5   6   7   8   9   10

Library of Congress Cataloging in Publication Data

Dolan, Paul J
    Of war and war's alarms.

    Bibliography: p.
    Includes index.
    1.   Fiction--19th century--History and criticism.
2.   Fiction--20th century--History and criticism.
3.   Politics in literature.   I.   Title.
PN3448.P6D6   1976   809.3'3   75-11287
ISBN 0-02-907500-9

Copyright Acknowledgments

for ISABEL . . .

POLITICS

In our time the destiny of man presents its meaning in political terms.

Thomas Mann

How can I, that girl standing there,
My attention fix
On Roman or on Russian
Or on Spanish politics?
Yet here's a travelled man that knows
What he talks about,
And there's a politician
That has read and thought,
And maybe what they say is true
Of war and war's alarms,
But O that I were young again
And held her in my arms !

William Butler Yeats
1939

Contents

Acknowledgments Personal

Many people helped the book to come to be, and I hereby cheerfully acknowledge my outstanding debts.

Joseph Carpino, Nino Langiulli, John McDermott, Francis X. Slade — philosophers, friends, teachers, colleagues — are responsible for most of the good ideas in the book but are in no way to blame for its faults.

Herbert Weisinger read an early draft of the manuscript with more patience, care, and wisdom than the premature effort deserved.

Peter Shaw, scholar and stylist, helped to sharpen the arguments.

Alfred Kazin was a thoughtful and very encouraging reader of a late draft.

Val Webb encouraged me to write the book I really wanted to.

Bob Wallace was a very patient editor.

Lillian Silkworth typed, read, and helped in many ways.

Joanna Kalinowski typed the bulk of the final manuscript swiftly and skillfully, and Phyllis Reed contributed a timely chapter in an hour of need.

I owe special thanks to the people and facilities of the

Library of the State University of New York at Stony Book
and the Hicksville Public Library for all their help.

Peter, John, and Paul II usually remembered to ask about
the progress of the manuscript.

The dedication says all the rest.

Chapter One

The Lamps of Europe

AT DUSK on the evening of the third of August 1914, Sir Edward Grey, the British foreign secretary, knowing that the German invasion of Belgium would begin in the morning, walked to the window of his Whitehall office, looked out over the darkening city and said, "The lamps are going out all over Europe; we shall not see them lit again in our lifetime."

He was right. Something did happen to Western civilization in 1914 and the great war of that year now seems only the first act of a great historical drama. The second act began in September 1939 and ended in 1945. Now, during an uneasy intermission, it is possible to examine the products of art in an effort to understand better the processes of history.

This book starts from the premise that serious fiction is one of the best places to learn about politics as a human experience. One of its assumptions is Ezra Pound's: that the artists are the antennae of the race. Another is that of Wyndham Lewis: the artist is engaged in writing the history of the future. In *My Kinsman, Major Molineux, The Possessed, The Princess Casamassima, Heart of Darkness, Nostromo, In the Penal Colony, Gladius Dei, Mario and the Magician,* and *Doctor Faustus,* the artists were the antennae of the race, accurately recording the terrible events of the present and the future. Had the men of power studied the writers of prose, the wars and murders might not have happened. Had the politicians read the novels and understood what they were saying, the lamps to which Sir Edward Grey referred might not have gone out. Those lights of Western bourgeois nationalism were extinguished in the struggles described by Hawthorne, Dostoyevsky, James, Conrad, Kafka and Mann: the moral conflicts of that will to power which led so many nations, so willingly, into the wars which consumed them.

A theme of this book is the clash of some of the imperatives familiar in the study of nineteenth- and twentieth-century history: nationalism and individual salvation occupy the American Hawthorne and the Russian Dostoyevsky; James deals with the conflict of class and conscience, and Conrad with the imperialist expansion of the white, northern European nations across the face of the globe. Kafka's vision is of a technocracy in which a human dimension to political action is no longer possible. Nazism and Mann loom large in this study because Nazi Germany was one kind of logical conclusion to the idea of the nation-state, and Mann's treatment of that state in *Doctor Faustus* is a logical conclusion to the idea of politics in a novel. Mann, who read Dostoyevsky and Conrad as he wrote *Doctor Faustus,* restates the problems of politics and morality, of art and humanity, with which they struggled. He writes, however, in the full realization that their prophecies have been fulfilled.

The nation-state is the product of Renaissance political thought and the systematic exploitation of technological power. The novel, another invention of the Renaissance mind, is the vehicle the modern consciousness created to reflect itself. Sooner or later the two creations of the age of individual assertion and individual doubt, of collective action and singular morality, had to become involved with each other, and fiction had to concern itself with the problems of citizenship. Having as its protagonist a man on a quest for a place in a world in which he does not completely believe, the novel could take as its special subject the experience of that man within and without a country. In the nineteenth and twentieth centuries, the creators of fiction turned to political questions; and, using all of the resources of their art, they, in R. P. Blackmur's phrase, added "to the stock of available reality."

Almost all of the authors of these works were themselves exiles, and they acted out in their lives as well as their works the moral problem of politics: that of treason and loyalty. These words, and all the sins and virtues they stand for, have a civic ring, but they are not limited to their civic meaning. Loyalty or treason in relation to the polis are the public counterparts of the individual actions by which we define ourselves as citizens of the city of God, or the city of man; as loyal subjects of a country, or of humanity. The clash of personal and political imperatives, the conflicts of the moral and the civic, the problems of belief and artistic responsibility—symbolized in part by the exiles of the authors—are the subjects of the novels and tales. Those subjects are the subject of this book.

A large segment of modern consciousness is embodied in political structures; these, in turn, shape and are shaped by that consciousness. So politics cannot be understood only as the political scientist, the historian, the economist, the sociologist, the psychologist, or even the philosopher understands it. The novel provides its special kind of knowledge because it deals with the conscious and unconscious experience of politics as a human, moral, psychological and aesthetic phenomenon. Fiction does not try to describe public deeds, but to create a self, aware that it is contending for a place in the world amid the clamor of conflicting demands for absolute loyalty. Conrad, for example, stirred by his own memories of revolutionary nationalism and by the accounts in the daily newspaper of American exploits in Panama, imagined the entire Western adventure in imperialism as the story of four or five people trying to live up to their visions of themselves. Kafka transformed his tortured dreams and the fate of Dreyfus into the history and mythology of a penal colony. Mann, in exile in America, seeking some metaphor to explain the moral blindness of the German people to the perversions of national socialism, allows incest, his own private symbol for his tortured experience, to stand for the mind of a people so turned in upon itself that it heard only its own most private promptings to madness.

The private experience of public conflict is the usual subject of fiction and this book deals with conflicts which were clearly political. The technique of Henry James illustrates the way in which fiction incorporates politics. James set out, in *The Princess Casamassima*, to write a book that would sell many copies so that he could become popular and rich. He chose a topic that seemed surefire: assassins and anarchists. Since a Russian czar and an American president had been assassinated just a few years before, and England was shocked and shaken by the mad Irish terrorists responsible for the Phoenix Park murders, this novel was likely to succeed. The book did not succeed as James had hoped; it became instead a book that makes more real to us the class and national hatreds that led to the series of assassinations which culminated in June 1914.

James' subject is the mind of his protagonist, Hyacinth Robinson, a pledged assassin who turns his pistol on himself rather than his designated victim because he can no longer sustain himself in his conflicting loyalties. Gavrilo Princip felt no such division of self and on June 28, 1914, he turned his pistol on the Archduke Francis Ferdinand and his wife Sophie of Austria-Hungary. James' record of Hyacinth's fine consciousness is a document in the history of events leading to Princip's act. James deals with the motives of a private and anonymous citizen whose sense of injustice makes it possible for him to step into the public world and change the course of history. Hyacinth cannot commit the political murder to which he pledged himself; but in showing his readers the public world of Europe in the Gilded Age and Hyacinth's awareness of it, James succeeds in showing that anarchism is not necessarily madness but is possibly an attempt at political redress. By compelling his reader to relive the pain of Hyacinth's choices, James makes anarchism more humanly understandable.

The public and private themes of *The Princess Casamassima* are, moreover, multidimensional. In writing a novel of topical interest, James' unconscious motive was to exorcise his sense of being, like his protagonist, an orphan. His feelings about the recent death of his parents are projected into Hyacinth's orphaned state; out of his problems with his overbearing brother William, he creates the character of Paul Muniment; and, to cope with his responses to his neurasthenic sister Alice, he creates Rosy Muniment as an invalid and a tyrant. Thus, James' own deep feelings of his disintegrated family incline him to the public theme of anarchism. His story of the isolated individual struggling with his personal, political, and aesthetic imperatives prefigures the fate of Europe.

Confusion about power and loyalty, individual and class, become part of the very shape of the fiction. The second book of *The Princess Casamassima* ends on a foggy London street with Hyacinth in a cab on his way to meet the legendary revolutionist, Hoffendahl, who will give him his fatal assignment.

> It was getting to be midnight; the drive seemed interminable to Hyacinth's impatience and curiosity. He sat next to Muniment, who passed a strong arm around him, holding him all the way as if for a tacit sign of indebtedness. This gave Hyacinth pleasure till he began to wonder if it mightn't represent also the instinct to make sure of him as against possible weak afterthoughts. They all ended by sitting silent

as the cab jogged along murky miles, and by the time it stopped our young man had wholly lost, in the drizzling gloom, a sense of their whereabouts.

Book Three begins, in some editions, on the facing page, as follows:

Hyacinth got up early—an operation attended with very little effort, as he had scarce closed his eyes all night. What he saw from his window made him dress as quickly as a young man might who desired more than ever that his appearance shouldn't give strange ideas about him. . . .

James is playing a cinematic trick upon the reader. The morning on which Hyacinth awakens is on the next page, but it is three months later; because the previous book ended in the middle of a night journey, the juxtaposition of Hyacinth and the morning is deliberately confusing. The sudden, deceptive shift in the narrative disorients the reader as Hyacinth himself is disoriented. On that morning at the opening of Book Three, Hyacinth is at Medley, visiting the Princess at her rented country house. He is confused because his journey has brought him to this lovely seat of leisurely virtues, and the oppositions which disturb Hyacinth, and the reader, are those between what Disraeli called the "two nations." Suddenly present on the facing pages are the dark night and foggy streets of the anarchists' plots for destruction and the sunny rooms and broad lawns of the spacious house, the repository of the aesthetic values of history. Hyacinth at Medley is only one page away from Hoffendahl, the chief of those who would destroy Medley; day and night, destruction and preservation—all of the confusion in Hyacinth's mind is meant to prefigure the confusion at the end of the book when in response to another invitation he is supposed to go as a guest to another noble house and murder his host. Then, completely divided against himself, Hyacinth commits suicide. But here, at the midpoint of the book, another kind of climax is intended.

In Book Three, at Medley, Hyacinth encounters a world he had not known before, a world worth preserving. The discovery of something innocently beautiful is the beginning of his fatal confusion. In the juxtaposition of Book Two and Book Three, the reader is, at first, more confused than Hyacinth on that morning and is, therefore, forced to get into Hyacinth's mind in order to straighten out the confusion. That is James' success as a novelist; his concern is not the contrast of rich and poor, nor the ironic biographies of the aristocrats among the anarchists, rather he wants to depict the forces contending for power in the world as they are present in Hyacinth's consciousness. James gives us these forces, the sinister and powerful, the comfortable and powerless, as they feel to his protagonist. As the reader lives through Hyacinth's experience, he understands as never before the human tragedy of the class war.

That is how political fiction makes its counterstatement to Plato's parable of the just state. In *The Republic*, Socrates offers to explain to Adeimantus the nature of justice by showing how the just state is the just man writ large. Political fiction reveals the injustice of the state in terms of the private consciousness of one person; or, in other words, with the crisis of the state as the crisis of an individual member. Politicians and philosophers deal with schema and with structures of governance. The novelist deals with a soul in pain because it cannot find its place in the structures; the question of justice is replaced by the question of survival.

In Hawthorne's story, *My Kinsman, Major Molineux*, Robin, the boy-hero, is almost destroyed because he assumes that the new world is to be run according to the same principles of privilege as had the old. Unknowingly, he walks into a revolution, but he is resourceful and learns quickly that the state has no other sanction than what those who have power give it and that his chance for success depends on his making peace with this real world. With a bang and a whimper the Puritan theocracy is finished.

In the *Walpurgisnacht* of his story, Hawthorne presents the American Revolution, the French Revolution and the triumph of Jacksonian Democracy, the second American revolution. He does all this by concentrating on the frightened, confused mind of a boy confronted with a martyr and a mob. Great dramas of modern political upheaval are acted out for the reader on the muddy streets of a New England village, early in the eighteenth century.

The protagonist—there are no heroes—in modern political fiction struggles to maintain his individual identity against the forces of collectivization for the right or left which more and more shape his world. He does not represent, like Macbeth or Lear, the condition of the state in his own person. He matters only to himself and to some few near to him who need him, or love him, or wish to use him. He is not, as in Shakespeare, the ruler of the state or even an attendant lord; rather, he is one who is conscious of being ruled by others and by events, conscious of power and powerlessness. As fiction replaced drama as the genre in which politics would be represented, the problem of the stature of the character was solved by the process of internalization inherent in the novel form. The characters, however bourgeois or insignificant, are conscious of the events in their lives, and the reader is conscious of the significance of those events beyond the lives in which they occur. Thus, Adrian Leverkuhn in *Doctor Faustus* is some part of Hitler; and the barren marriage of Charles and Emilia Gould in *Nostromo* shows clearly that the rape of peoples and the earth, in history called imperialism, could not sustain itself no matter how noble its aspirations. The characters who are obsessed are related to all of the political assassins of the last hundred years who have proved that no man is so insignificant or so powerless that he cannot extend himself with the technological power of a weapon and alter the course of history. Through the actors in political novels, the reader becomes a participant in the re-creation of reality which is the making of history.

Machiavelli defined modern political consciousness with his description of the state as an order made by men subject only to the sanction of men. The Glorious Revolution, the American Revolution, the French Revolution, 1830 and 1848, Russia in 1905 and 1917, and the examples of Napoleon, Hitler and Stalin have made clear the meaning of that definition. In the last two centuries, human absolutes have clearly replaced theological models, and history can be seen as a struggle between revolutionary democracy and total tyranny. Some artists have, in this time, depicted men and women trying to place themselves in the world of power politics, a world without theological or moral sanctions. The artists have re-created the world of *sauve qui peut* and, for the individual, the problem of being a moral man in an indifferent state.

It is possible to describe the development of Western nations since Machiavelli in terms of dramatic motivations. The purpose of a nation has been to secure and sustain power; to secure and sustain a place in the world of nations. The means to that end are extension and expansion. Hitler could, therefore, silence his adversaries by telling them, in their own language, that he planned only the expansion necessary to insure German security. An individual acts out that same motivation and recapitulates in his life the national drama. In growing up, he makes a place for himself in the world, acts to keep that place secure, and tries to sustain himself in a community of individuals. Thus, individual and nation act in each other's drama.

Political philosophy describes the nature of that "interaction" in language appropriate to its theoretical concerns. Political fiction creates the feeling of being an actor in two simultaneous and sometimes conflicting scenarios. Political philosophy considers the questions of legitimacy and the transmission of power because, as Machiavelli observed, the real problem is power: how to get it; how to keep it. Political fiction is also concerned with these questions, but finds for them their artistic correlative, an intellectual and emotional symbol for the complex human feelings about such legitimacy and transmission. That is why parricide is such a consistent concern in political fiction. The idea of parricide stands for the real feelings of power, powerlessness, and the urge to violence that comes when someone tries to create his own place of power.

Thus, Hawthorne tells his story of the coming of age of America, the first "new" nation of the modern world, in terms of a boy's participation in the ritual slaying of his father's brother who also represents the parental authority of England in the recalcitrant colonies. Robin finds and loses his kinsman but discovers new meanings of "kinsman" in the midst of revolutionary turmoil. He survives the failure of transmission of power across a generation which is the final failure of any political order. Others, in other stories, fare differently, but the failure itself is a constant theme in political fiction. Hyacinth Robinson, for example, not only has real parents and a legacy from them with which he must come to terms, but has a host of surrogate parents trying to impose on him systems of value, personal and political. Hyacinth is not only called upon to slay his father; he must find him among all the pretenders to that title.

In Conrad's *Heart of Darkness*, Kurtz becomes bestial when he tyrannizes those who love him, those whom he had regarded as his children. Nostromo, in his book, is slain by Viola, the old Garibaldino, the man who regarded Nostromo as his son and heir and who was destined to be his father-in-law. In the manner of some parents, he slays the son who does not act as he had wished. Charles Gould, in the same novel, scores his hollow triumph over the warning ghost of his father. A central symbol in Kafka's *In the Penal Colony* is the change in the political order from the Old Commandant to the New Commandant. The officer in that story dies wishing for the return of the stern old ruler who knew so well what was good for the children. Adrian Leverkuhn, in *Doc-

tor Faustus, must go beyond his father's modest efforts to "speculate the elements." Adrian must slay Beethoven and take back the Ninth Symphony; that act represents the total perversion of the Western tradition that was nazism. In the process he also destroys the child, Echo, who is his only possibility for human feeling. His destruction of his artist-father and his nephew-son stands for the impulse that created a political order to destroy the meaning of political order.

Of the great novelists who have been involved with the struggle of generations as a political metaphor, none is more involved than Dostoyevsky. *The Possessed* is a study of generations and Dostoyevsky's public theme is the progress from spineless liberalism to the horrors of nihilism. In pursuit of that public theme, he vilifies Turgenev as one of the spineless liberals in the character of Karamazinov; and *The Possessed* is, in one sense, Dostoyevsky's rewriting of Turgenev's novel of the generations, *Fathers and Sons*. It is, however, from Dostoyevsky's private vision that the power of *The Possessed* derives. He uses his own nightmares of parricide and child molestation to represent the horrors of an unredeemed political order in much the same way as Mann uses the theme of incest in *Doctor Faustus*. The villains are the anarchists, and they are the slayers of parents and the corrupters of children. They are beyond salvation and so is a world in which they inherit the power. In *The Possessed*, Dostoyevsky comes close to saying that the political degeneration he envisions is a matter of simple heredity, and he exploits his drama of the generations for his own kind of messianic politics.

Parricide in some form has had, since Sophocles' *Oedipus*, a double fascination for the writer of political fiction. It is, first of all, a mythic concern for all men. It is also a symbol for the problem of succession in the political order. Thus, it can stand for both the personal and the public thrusts to power which characterize the time in which the political fiction to be studied here was produced. In that time, roughly 1830 to 1948, the world was engaged in a furious arms race which culminated in nuclear weapons. This era of national expansion is sometimes called "the age of ideology," but the ideologies were justifications for the exercise of power or explanations of the state of powerlessness. The political fiction of the period deals with individual human responses to the rampant demands for national expression. These responses were learned, apparently, in childhood and are the strategies of survival. The political question at the end of the psychological consideration is whether there is any chance for individual morality in a world more and more devoted to the instruments and exercises of power.

Fiction and politics do meet in ways that are important to both, and the artist attempts, like Socrates, to talk about the nature of the just man in a just state. The protagonists in the novels and tales seek some sanction for their lives beyond success; they seek for some authenticity in themselves. As an alternative to the systematic application of power, a political order may be imagined as a sum of moral arrangements. Where politics is not such a sum, the problem for the individual is that of maintaining for himself the possibility of moral arrangements when the public world is designed, at best, to be indifferent to them. That incongruity, conflict, clash is the stuff of drama and in political fiction the problematic is the loyalty of the protagonist in a divided world. Each must, like Robin at one end and Adrian at another, face the commanding question: with what am I to identify myself—church or state, country or class, nation or family, friend or comrade, men or God, sense of self or sense of duty, deepest feeling or overpowering idea? The presumption is that the social order is not in harmony and the pairs are not congruent.

In an ideal political order, public and private demands upon the citizen could be balanced in justice, and the citizen would be at peace with himself and with his world. Novelists, however, create imaginary worlds with real political problems in them so their characters know turmoil, not peace. To the general task in fiction of rendering a growth of consciousness, the political novelist adds the particular question of citizenship, of identity within and without a state. Knowing that what a man identifies with will sooner or later become his identity, to whom or to what is Robin, or Marlow, or Nostromo, or the Explorer to be loyal? Martin Decoud and Charles Gould, citizen expatriate and resident alien, act out their private tragedies of blindness, and they represent to the reader the tragedies of blindness called nationalism and imperialism. Nikolai Stavrogin, a quintessential Russian character, cannot solve his problems of allegiance and dies, a suicide, as a citizen of the Canton of Uri.

This book is an "essay," a consideration of a cluster of works having some common concerns. The novels and tales raise questions, familiar to twentieth-century readers, of maintaining a conviction of morality and a certainty of citizenship. Hawthorne, Dostoyevsky, James, Conrad, Kafka and Mann used fiction to explore their own painful consciousness of politics in the modern world, and this book is an attempt to go with them on their explorations. Ezra Pound, quoting Flaubert, said that if the French had read properly *L'Education sentimentale*, they could have avoided the debacle of 1870. The writers considered here give a special insight into the moral nature of our civic and psychological states which, if studied properly, might help to prevent yet another debacle.

Neither Pound nor Flaubert was merely whimsical. Art is essential to politics because the ruler can only rule the kingdom which he imagines, and the citizens will hold the leader responsible only insofar as they have a vital idea of what their state should be. It was natural for Aristotle to write a *Politics* and base his *Poetics* on a play about a tyrant; the artist and the ruler both imagine a state and then try to realize it. Prospero, for example, must first re-create in his own mind the responsibilities of the ruler, and then purge the imagination of his usurping brother before peace and justice are restored. The connection of art and politics is an ancient and honorable one. One purpose of fiction is to expand the moral imagination of its readers. Made more aware of the complexities of human desires, the citizen can make more appropriate demands upon himself and upon his commonwealth.

Politics is, unfortunately, no longer the high art it was; nor is political fiction the same engaging moral forum it once was. We seem to be trapped in the legacy of the moral and political failures presented in the fiction of Hawthorne, Conrad, and Mann. Indeed, the sordid scandal of Watergate and the tapes preserved as a record of performance reveal the terrible poverty of Richard Nixon's imagination. He imagined a nation of petty thieves with himself at its head. In Russia, China and India, the problem of organizing life for numbers of citizens on a scale never even dreamed of seems to have swamped any sense of political possibility that is not quantitative. So, these books presume a relation of the political and the moral which may not be tenable for too much longer. If that is the case, then it is tragic.

I write as an American born in the middle of the third decade of the twentieth century and it would be foolish for me to pretend that my understanding of politics, theoretical or practical, would ever get far from those roots. In writing about the re-creation of political realities in art, I write as a pragmatist, a democrat and a Democrat. I am a moderate socialist, hopeful about the possibility of the triumph of democratic socialism but skeptical of all human systems. In art and politics I try not to look for answers or attitudes but to look for and to cultivate what Henry James called "the penetrating imagination." In his Preface to *The Princess Casamassima*, he wrote:

> What it all came back to was, no doubt, something like *this* wisdom—that if you haven't, for fiction, the root of the matter in you, haven't the sense of life and the penetrating imagination, you are a fool in the very presence of the revealed and assured; but that if you *are* so armed you are not really help-

less, not without your resource, even before mysteries abysmal.

So armed, I continue to believe that there is a connection between morality and politics and that I, and others, will continue to act upon that premise.

It was Cervantes who bequeathed to Western fiction its special task: to depict the struggle of the individual consciousness to define, to defend, and to preserve its identity in a changing social order with which it must somehow come to terms. A handful of artists, beginning in the nineteenth century, recognized that classes and nations were engaged in the same drama of self-determination, self-preservation, and self-expression as were individuals, and with the same tragic consequences. These artists made their stories of both the tragic actor and his nation. They doubled Socrates' task and wrote the large in the small and the small in the large.

Sir Edward Grey certainly did not know Franz Kafka, a citizen of a hostile state. He would have understood, however, Kafka's judgment that the war "arose above all from a monstrous lack of imagination." Sir Edward Grey knew, as he stood thinking about the horror that had finally begun, that the forces of darkness had overtaken all the plans of men and the slouching beast had been let loose.

Chapter Two

Hawthorne: The Politics of Puberty

AT THE CLIMAX of *My Kinsman, Major Molineux*, the Major is driven in a tumbril by a revolutionary mob past his frightened nephew, Robin, and at that moment the reader is simultaneously on the streets of a New England village on the eve of the American Revolution and in the gutters of Paris at the height of the terror. The doubling of the emotional setting of the story is Hawthorne's indication that he wants his parable of Robin's coming of age also to stand for the basic sense of politics in the modern world, the sense of a soul in a chaotic cosmos.

Prefixed to the story of Robin, the boy who sets out to find his kinsman and his fate, is a paragraph of historical background. With its official, impersonal tone, this opening paragraph seems separate from the story which follows in a way that often puzzles readers.

> After the Kings of Great Britain had assumed the right of appointing the colonial Governors, the measures of the latter seldom met with the ready and general approbation which had been paid to those of their predecessors, under the origi-

nal charters. The people looked with most jealous scrutiny to the exercise of power which did not emanate from themselves, and they usually rewarded their rulers with slender gratitude for the compliances by which, in softening their instructions from beyond the sea, they had incurred the reprehension of those who gave them. The annals of Massachusetts Bay will inform us that of six Governors in the space of about forty years from the surrender of the old charter, under James II, two were imprisoned by a popular insurrection; a third, as Hutchinson inclines to believe, was driven from the province by the whizzing of a musket ball; a fourth, in the opinion of the same historian, was hastened to his grave by continual bickerings with the House of Representatives; and the remaining two, as well as their successors, till the Revolution, were favored with few and brief intervals of peaceful sway. The inferior members of the court party, in times of high political excitement, led scarcely a more desirable life. These remarks may serve as a preface to the following adventures, which chanced upon a summer night, not far from a hundred years ago. The reader, in order to avoid a long and dry detail of colonial affairs, is requested to dispense with an account of the train of circumstances that had caused much temporary inflammation of the popular mind.

Revolution is the theme of the first paragraph and it is in terms of a revolution that Hawthorne wants us to see Robin's story, the strange events of a summer night. Like the frame of *Heart of Darkness*, the scene aboard the *Nellie*, this opening provides the necessary historical and social setting for the story of an individual quest; for both Hawthorne and Conrad the two are inseparable.

Two revolutions are cited in the opening paragraph of *My Kinsman, Major Molineux;* the first is the assumption by the "kings of Great Britain" of the right to appoint colonial governors, an act of supererogation of the original charters. The second is the series of responses of the colonials to this act of arbitrary power. The clue provided is that revolution itself is a dominant theme in the story; and Hawthorne is writing about the French and American Revolutions and, indirectly, about the more recent triumph of Jacksonianism and the defeat of John Quincy Adams, which marked the end of the New England aristocracy as a force in American political life. Hawthorne's theme, embodied in his story of a boy's quest, is that of coming of age in the modern world, in full recognition that this process is continuous for a nation as well as an individual, and that finding one's place is almost impossible because the revolutionary nature of modern politics keeps obliterating the place to which one aspired.

Any work of fiction involves the manipulation of the expectations and responses of its readers. We are alternately engaged and rebuffed, satisfied and frustrated, as the events move to a conclusion; in the process, if the story is worthwhile, we are deeply, personally engaged with the material. Kenneth Burke has described what he calls the "strategies" of the author and the "equations" of the work. Simply put, Burke's position, and mine, is that the work is designed to have an effect on the reader; that words are chosen and placed first to involve the reader in the sequence of events and, thereby, to alter his perceptions of himself and his world.

Hawthorne's "strategy" in the opening paragraph is to remind his readers of the history of colonial rebellions which were steps toward the American Revolution. He does not want to deal with that cataclysmic event, but he wants to incorporate the idea of it as a setting for the actions of his characters. So, in this almost pedantic first paragraph in which Hawthorne seems too impatient to be artistic, he is manipulating the expectations of his readers. They will know the central event at the end of the progression he describes and will, on that basis, make a psychological investment of themselves in seeing the story through to its conclusion. Having set in motion the sequence, Hawthorne can, in the remarkable calculus of art, focus on one segment of the sequence to tell his story. Knowing that his readers would regard the

American Revolution with piety, Hawthorne manipulates that anticipated response to produce the disturbing identification of the American and French Revolutions at the climax of his story. And, to complete for now the discussion of "strategies," it is in creating his image of the fallen major as Christ that Hawthorne plays the patriotic against the religious response to achieve that uneasy balance in which the reader cannot give himself to some previously determined response. The strategies and equations of a serious work of art engage, distract, teach, and finally change us.

Having established his political base in the opening paragraph, Hawthorne proceeds to his story, the old one of a young man seeking his place in society. *My Kinsman, Major Molineux* has, however, a special dimension: the specifically political nature of that society becomes part of the question of the place of the protagonist. Hawthorne, and a handful of other writers who came after him, saw that the political order in which the quest for identity took place altered the very nature of that quest. In setting the story of Robin against the preliminary skirmishes of the American Revolution, Hawthorne created a major text in modern political fiction.

My Kinsman, Major Molineux is two stories that reflect each other: a boy begins to become a man and a colony begins to be a nation. The human pain and the moral ambiguity attendant upon both processes is the subject of this story and of political fiction. Hawthorne is able to tell both stories simultaneously because he concentrates on what Aristotle said the dramatist must put first: the plot. *My Kinsman, Major Molineux* is, in fact, similar to the plot of the play from which Aristotle derived his definition of dramatic form and purpose, Sophocles' *Oedipus*. Both the Greek drama and the American story involve a quest in which the protagonist sets out to find a person. The quest is neither arbitrary nor merely personal; both Oedipus and Robin believe, in beginning their search, that they must find that person to insure their own well-being. Oedipus discovers that the guilty man he seeks is himself, and, in the process, learns about himself and the nature of the universe. In completing his search, Robin, like Oedipus, finds that his kinsman is not the man he had expected and that the completion of his search is not a resolution, but shocking knowledge and an unexpected necessity of choice. In the story of Robin's quest, he and his readers learn something about the nature of loyalty, citizenship, and moral action in the making of a modern nation.

It is easy to see, in retrospect, how the plot unifies the story of Robin and the American experience, but that is only because the "equations" in the story work so well. Robin's motive is made clear in the second paragraph: he wants to find his kinsman because he will provide for him a place in the new world. Without the prologue of the first paragraph, *My Kinsman, Major Molineux* would seem a story like Shirley Jackson's *The Lottery*, an allegory and a ritual tale to be understood primarily in psychological and anthropological terms. But the major is both a personal relation and a political figure, and Hawthorne is concerned with the morality of history; or, perhaps, what a lapsed Puritan would regard as the profanity of history. Religion, psychology, myth, ritual, and superstition are all part of the story, but politics is paramount. "London" and "New England" are juxtaposed in the third paragraph; the tavern in which Robin first encounters "the devil" has as its sign the figure of a "British hero." The political statement of the plot is: to find my kinsman and join him with whom I am most closely identified. Thus, Robin's private quest is analogous to that of the citizens of the town and the country they represent. They, too, had come across the water to make a new life in a different land. They, too, are in the process of discovering the meaning of the word, "kinsman."

Robin's story begins with his crossing a river in the darkness of night on an ominous ferry for which he pays a heavy fare. Resolutely, he sets out to find his kinsman but has, instead, only a series of disturbing encounters. First, there is the world: the city with its lights, inhabitants, streets crowded or deserted, and the ships which lead to all the places on the globe. Then, in the tavern, Robin meets the devil: "His features were separately striking almost to grotesqueness, and the whole face left a deep impression on the memory. The forehead bulged out into a double prominence, with a vale between; the nose came boldly forth in an irregular curve, and its bridge was of more than a finger's breadth; the eyebrows were deep and shaggy, and the eyes glowed beneath them like fire in a cave." Robin is to encounter this threatening man twice more during the evening, the last time as the leader of the unholy procession for Robin's kinsman, the major.

Having seen the world and the devil, Robin next encounters the flesh. The scarlet petticoat and sparkling eyes of the prostitute stand out in the uncertain darkness of the story as do details in dreams. The saucy wench completes the trilogy of world, flesh, and devil that Robin encounters in his quest, and a reader of Puritan allegories would know that only doubtful good could come from such a fair of vanities. The three traditional symbols stand for fallen humanity. The implication is that those who make a revolution are those who have already become the party of sin.

The dream quality is itself a complicated part of Hawthorne's control of his audience. Robin's quest involves his "dream" in the sense of that word as goal, or place, or happiness. The reader watches as that dream turns literally to nightmare. The dream of the boy for making his fortune has a counterpart in the story: that of the patriots of taking their place as a new nation in the world. That dream must also, it seems, become nightmare before it is realized.

After his encounter with the girl, Robin meets groups in "outlandish attire" hurrying by. They are, we later discover, on their way to the tarring of the major. They address Robin (they are the first people to speak to him before his questioning), but they speak in passwords and then curse Robin very plainly when he cannot respond. Robin's problem in speaking to the citizens of the town is an important symbol in the story: although this is ostensibly his country, Robin cannot speak the language. Here he obviously does not know the words and elsewhere he has found that his words do not have the effect he intends. His enquiries about Major Molineux are treated as curses or affronts even though he intends them to command respect. Not knowing the language is an aspect of Robin's entrance into a new country and an early example of the Orwellian principle that a change in the political order means a change in the language. Robin's problem of communication is finally solved in the wordless tableau of the major in the cart when Robin sees and understands.

Another kind of communication takes place when Robin peers into the deserted church. A ray of moonlight falls upon an open Bible in the same paragraph in which the distant rumblings of the mob are first heard. The empty church seems both hushed and holy, "because no earthly and impure feet were within the walls." Those impure feet are, however, approaching. The contrast of the sacred and peaceful with the political and turbulent is another equation by means of which Hawthorne controls his stories of Robin's coming of age and the making of America. The contrast is characteristic of virtually all political fiction.

In the climactic scene of *My Kinsman, Major Molineux*, the *Walpurgisnacht* in which Robin finds the kinsman he has sought, the tumultuous procession, led by the man with the horned forehead, in military attire, his face now black and red, prefigures the revolution that is to come: "The single horseman, clad in a military dress, and bearing a drawn sword, rode onward as the leader, and, by his fierce and variegated countenance, appeared like war personified; the red of one cheek was an emblem of fire and sword; the blackness of the other betokened the mourning that attends them." (This strange figure bears, in his many incarnations, some faint resemblance to Andrew Jackson, conqueror of the

British and leader of a popular "revolution.") In making this *Walpurgisnacht* the prototype of revolution, Hawthorne is saying more than that the American Revolution was grotesque in a way not usually understood by Americans. He is not simply deploring the vandalism of democracy upon the dignity of the old order. The reader is, rather, like Robin, entangled in the drama of conflicting feelings.

Hawthorne manipulates the expectations of his readers in order to shock them into new awareness. Hawthorne, and his readers, believe in the justice of the American Revolution and its consequences. The story of Robin is, however, the story of one boy's experience of that revolution as a personal crisis, not an historical event. The revolution to which so many innocent sleepers in the town are awakened embodies some corruptions. Patriotism may or may not be the last refuge of a scoundrel, but violent political movements will always provide a home for scoundrels. The point of the story is not to be unpatriotic or blasphemous or to correct the simple pieties of national history. The cause of independence remains a good cause, whether it is personal for Robin or national for the citizens; and the New World across the water, the world of New Canaan, Providence, and Concord, is still the New World. Hawthorne, nevertheless, makes us contemplate what happens to a good cause when it is embraced by ordinary human beings.

The confrontation of Robin and the major is arranged so that Hawthorne gains for the boy and the man the sympathy necessary for his story to succeed. The scene is a counterweight, in its palpable agony, to both Robin's priggish ambition and the presumptively positive response of an American audience to the overthrow of a British ruler. Robin's pride and place seeking are as much a part of the old order as the major's position. Even though both are to be purged in the revolution, we must have some human sympathy for them if we are to understand the moral ambiguities of political action with which the story is concerned. On a natural level we are

moved to sympathy for the major by the qualities of his character evident in this hour of trial:

> He was an elderly man, of large and majestic person, and
> strong, square features betokening a steady soul; but steady
> as it was, his enemies had found means to shake it. His
> face was pale as death, and far more ghastly; the broad fore-
> head was contracted in his agony, so that his eyebrows
> formed one grizzled line; his eyes were red and wild, and the
> foam hung white upon his quivering lip. His whole frame
> was agitated by a quick and continued tremor, which his
> pride strove to quell, even in those circumstances of over-
> whelming humiliation. But perhaps the bitterest pang of all
> was when his eyes met those of Robin; for he evidently knew
> him on the instant, as the youth stood witnessing the foul
> disgrace of a head grown gray in honor.

The reader is meant to know Robin's pain at that moment.
The shrewd boy has not been an especially likable character
up to this point, but he is now just a boy faced with a terrible
question of loyalty and survival.

On a symbolic level, this witches' parade is a blasphemous
parody of the events of Holy Thursday night and the tarred-
and-feathered major a type of the mocked Christ. Robin,
faced with a choice, becomes St. Peter and denies the man he
had claimed as his savior. His laugh links him with the hysterical gaiety of the crowd and he is an outsider no longer.

Having found his kinsman in the midst of a frightening
spectacle that resembles in part an election night parade,
Robin is baffled and confused. Given the moral ambiguities
of the story, no other kind of conclusion is possible. Robin
had to deny the major to avoid sharing his fate, but the
Christ-like presentation of the major confuses our response
to Robin's act of self-preservation. To survive, Robin cuts his
tie to his rich relative and becomes a free and independent
man. In the same way, his country had to sever its tie to
England. No blame or praise is to be given. Hawthorne has
won from us some sympathy for the old order which per-

ished; the new order took care of itself in the writing of history. Robin, and the reader, have experienced fully the terrifying dimensions of E. M. Forster's famous statement on the problem of conscience and citizenship: "I hate the idea of causes, and if I had to choose between betraying my country and betraying my friend, I hope I should have the guts to betray my country." Hawthorne's story renders all the complexity, doubt, resolution, and ambiguity of Forster's "hope."

In the course of completing his quest, Robin learns a great deal about himself and the new country in which he must make his way. At first, ashamed of what he has done, he wishes to flee. But the kindly old man who has watched with him suggests that he stay and try again to find his place in the world, "Perhaps, as you are a shrewd youth, you may rise in the world without the help of your kinsman, Major Molineux." History belongs to those who survive their choices between the personal and the political. Tomorrow, Robin and his new country will set out to rise in the world.

The clearest question in political fiction is the question of loyalty; or, to give it its civic name, citizenship. Robin faces the question of his citizenship: in the old order of aristocracy and privilege or in the new, raw, and terrifying democracy with its uncertain promise. Hawthorne drew on his own deepest feelings about democracy in the creation of Robin's experience in the same way he drew upon his own recollected feelings of his journey, at fifteen, from his home in Maine to his appointed sojourn in the bustling town of Salem. Robin's laugh is his passport into the country to which his quest has unwittingly brought him. The climax of the story is the moment of choice represented by Robin's laugh at the spectacle of his uncle in the cart. The attendant moral-political problems inform all of the works with which this book is concerned.

How are the protagonists to declare their citizenship and what kind of psychological, moral, and even aesthetic elements are involved in the choice? The characters first define

to themselves their alternatives: am I to be a citizen of the
city of man, or the city of God; of the country of England, or
the realm of the oppressed; of the established political order,
or of the ideological vision of what might be? Then comes
the choice and its consequences. Political fiction gives us men
and women caught up in the pain of the questions and the
agony of the choice.

Robin at the tumbril makes his choice, and in that moment
all the major themes of modern political fiction are present.
The scene includes politics as inverted religion, the relation
of generation to generation, the morality of violent revolution,
and the question of personal authenticity as the price of
political success. Each of these themes appears again and
again in the narratives of man as a political animal.

The religious theme in *My Kinsman, Major Molineux* is important personally to the author. Hawthorne was aware of
himself as a New England man, heir to the remnants of the
Puritan theocracy. The idea of political persecution by those
assured of the purity of their own motives haunted him.
Writing of his own ancestors in the essay prefixed to *The
Scarlet Letter, The Custom House,* he said:

And yet, though invariably happiest elsewhere, there is
within me a feeling for old Salem, which, in lack of a better
phrase, I must be content to call affection. The sentiment is
probably assignable to the deep and aged roots which my
family has struck into the soil. It is now nearly two centuries
and a quarter since the original Briton, the earliest emigrant
of my name, made his appearance in the wild and forest-
bordered settlement, which has since become a city. . . .

The figure of that first ancestor, invested by family tradition with a dim and dusky grandeur, was present to my boy-
ish imagination, as far back as I can remember. It still haunts
me, and induces a sort of home-feeling with the past, which
I scarcely claim in reference to the present phase of the town.
I seem to have a stronger claim to a residence here on account of this grave, bearded, sable-cloaked and steeple-

crowned progenitor,—who came so early, with his Bible and
his sword, and trode the unworn street with such a stately
port, and made so large a figure, as a man of war and peace,
—a stronger claim than for myself, whose name is seldom
heard and my face hardly known. He was a soldier, legisla-
tor, judge; he was a ruler in the Church; he had all the Puri-
tanic traits, both good and evil. He was likewise a bitter
persecutor, as witness the Quakers, who have remembered
him in their histories, and relate an incident of his hard
severity towards a woman of their sect, which will last
longer, it is to be feared, than any record of his better deeds,
although these were many. His son, too, inherited the perse-
cuting spirit, and made himself so conspicuous in the martyrdom of the witches, that their blood may fairly be said to
have left a stain upon him. . . . At all events, I, the present
writer, as their representative, hereby take shame upon myself for their sakes, and pray that any curse incurred by
them . . . may be now and henceforth removed.

The sympathy for the major and the religious feeling in the
scene of his martyrdom by the mob are deeply felt by Hawthorne. He knows how zeal can lead to persecution and the
unsolvable dilemma of Robin, loyalty to family or self, is
realized partially because Hawthorne's story involves some
repudiation of his ancestors and he feels that pain.

The weaving into the story of encounters with the world,
the flesh and the devil, the analogy of the major to Christ and
Robin to St. Peter, and the light upon the Bible in the empty
church, in front of which the Witches' Sabbath-Election Night
Parade will pass, is Hawthorne's way of manipulating the
religious assumptions of his readers in this political tale of
zeal and righteous persecution. The idea with which Hawthorne works, and it is not limited to Hawthorne, to America
in 1830, or to the Puritan theocratic state, is that there is an
order—for the believer, a specific religious order—which en-
compasses and justifies the political order. Western political
thought has been haunted by the ghostly paradigm of a City
of God, the shadowy belief that a just political order reflects

in its most mundane operations the pattern of how men ought to be governed by each other. In Hawthorne, the heir of the Puritans and descendant of those who could persecute in the name of the kingdom of God on earth, that ghost was almost palpable.

Since Machiavelli, of course, the idea of such a religious, or even moral, order which political reality must reflect has been more openly abandoned for the recognition of political organization as self-sustaining power, and force and flattery have replaced moral philosophy in the description of states. But for Hawthorne, and the other writers considered here, the old belief dies hard; it remains a useful metaphor for the kind of personal justification of political action each character wants. The result for fiction is the creation of a character like Shatov in *The Possessed* who wants desperately to believe in some justification for his existence; or like Robin, who would prefer the innocence of conviction to the realities of doubt.

Robin loses his innocence when he discovers that no state, aristocratic or democratic, has the kind of paradigmatic justification which would make loyalty easy. Part of Hawthorne's irony in treating the material of the story is the conclusion that the only justification for political action is pragmatic: "Where treason flourishes, none dare call it treason." In *My Kinsman, Major Molineux*, the empty church and the new Holy Thursday ritual indicate that in the making of a nation it is necessary temporarily to suspend one's reliance on the Almighty because the work of revolution, even a good revolution, is the devil's task. Because Hawthorne is an artist writing fiction and not political philosophy, there is no theoretical discussion of the need for a willing suspension of values in order to remake the world. We have, instead, Robin's existential sense that piety is not enough—a first lesson in the American principle of the separation of church and state. Robin is "saved" by choosing the world of men.

In addition to the question of politics and salvation (or, if you will, dissent and survival), *My Kinsman, Major Molineux* embodies another of the pervasive concerns of modern political fiction, the war of the generations. The story is about Robin's coming of age, the symbolic slaying of his father and solving the initiation riddles so that he can take his place in society. Robin ends his dependence on an almighty parent figure as the rebels suspend their dependence on the ways of God. I have no desire to slight that interpretation of the story, but wish to emphasize the analogues of the personal and the public stories.

The biological fact with which a political order is meant to cope is that each new generation will make its own place in the social order and, therefore, in even the most stable societies, some displacement is inevitable. A political order is established to ensure maximum stability and minimum displacement; to make efficient the transition from one generation to another. Since no political order is perfect, however, conflict is inevitable between those who have come of age and those coming of age, between those in power and those who must assume power. Robin, caught in the conflict, declares himself independent of family in the same process by which the colony declares itself independent of the parent nation.

There is, I think, a biological analogue for this process of replacement and displacement. Beneath our conscious awareness of ourselves, cells replace cells constantly, creating anew the skin and organs with which we experience the world. It is possible to imagine a nation state, or any political order, undergoing the same invisible process of transformation. If we posit for only a moment, a self-conscious cell, aware of the process to which it is subject and, even perhaps, reluctant to participate in it, we have an analogue for the struggle of the generations: private and public, familial and political. It seems now no accident that Aristotle, the philosopher of politics and poetry, was a biologist.

Political fiction focuses on the problem of transmission

from generation to generation, on the conflict between those
who wish to preserve and those who wish to change. Robin
survives because he adapts but we are uneasy in his survival
because it involves parricide and regicide. Robin denies his
surrogate father, the major, when he realizes that his own
security is not in the hands of the major, but in those in whose
hands the major is. In the ambiguous climax of *My Kinsman,
Major Molineux*, Robin throws off the yoke of family as the
mob is throwing off the yoke of colony, but part of the irony
of that climax is that Robin had wanted to claim his family
connections for base motives and denies them when some
form of human sympathy seems called for. In that moment of
pain, when sympathy requires an heroic effort of which the
boy is not capable, Robin acts out his coming of age: he
learns that no person has in him virtue because of his birth.
Robin must recognize and choose what is virtue for him and
his experience stands for the experience of politics in the
real world: seeing in the midst of the turmoil, choosing in the
midst of the lynching. Only in art, with its penetrating imagination, can this feeling of impelled choices be made clear to
us.

Hawthorne is careful to set his tale in the early eighteenth
century amid the colonial rumblings which prefigured the
American Revolution. He is writing a tale, not a novel, and
the focus is on one boy in one night. Yet the reader is aware
that the events described do represent the American Revolution. An American reader, however, has some difficulty in
recognizing his revolution because with mob and tumbril it
seems more like the revolution that occurred in the gutters of
Paris than that in the fields of Concord. The conservative and
semirural American war for independence is linked with the
radical and urban French experience because Hawthorne is
exploiting a myth. In modern mythology the American was
the "better" of the two revolutions. It led directly to democratic government and was not marred by the horrors of the
terror or the subsequent relapse into tyranny. (Carlyle's *The*

French Revolution, almost exactly contemporary with *My Kinsman, Major Molineux,* is both a product of and purveyor of the mythological assumptions—as, indeed, is *A Tale of Two Cities.*) Hawthorne's point is that for individuals mythology does not work. The direct human experience of revolution is of personal violence and the necessity of choice without moral sanction. The artist is concerned with that human experience, not with historical differences among revolutions.

Violent displacement is the meaning of revolution. As the Professor says, in Conrad's *The Secret Agent,* "The condemned social order has not been built up on paper and ink, and I don't fancy that a combination of paper and ink will ever put an end to it." How, then, is the novelist to cope with violence? His protagonist cannot be a violent man or he loses the sympathy of the reader. (Notice, however, how Hawthorne establishes from the very beginning of the story Robin's potential for violence.) The protagonist must have the doubts of Hyacinth Robinson, the agony of Stavrogin, or must undergo the conversion of Kurtz. The character who begins with a commitment to violence is a Peter Verkhovensky and, however fascinating his machinations, we hate him. The problem of the artist is like that of the political theoretician. What, if anything, justifies violence is the theoretical question; the artistic one is how does the artist render sympathetically a character caught up in revolutionary violence? In fiction, some tragic choice must be involved and, therefore, characters in political fiction become the victims of violence not simply because their creators tend to be antirevolutionary. In the post-Machiavellian world of secular politics, there can be no Aeneas killing with divine sanction; if a protagonist takes up a sword, he will perish by that sword.

The political justification of violence is ideology: the idea of the good state must be brought to reality and, if violence is necessary, so be it. Lenin's famous aphorism that an omelet requires broken eggs is the summary of this position. Robin comes early in the age of ideology and participates in the

crude effort to make an ideology prevail. Hawthorne was in-
dicating the path others would take in creating fiction concerned with the problems of ideology and individual human
action. (The fact that so many of the writers discussed in this
book were exiles is testimony to the fact that the conflict of
ideology and individuality was not merely theoretic.) Ideology and individuality become, in political fiction, the poles
of the tragic choice.

Facing the mob, Robin makes his choice: by denying the
kinsman he sought, he becomes part of the new generation in
the new land and will now find his way without the aristocratic preference he expected. Robin's story is, after all, that
basic fable of the boy who leaves home to seek his fortune in
the world, the "success story." Robin learns that his worldly
success depends on neither God nor his ancestors, but upon
his coming to terms with the current political order. Many of
Robin's fictional descendants face the question of worldly
success; *Heart of Darkness* is, in one sense, the ultimate ironic
treatment of the young man's quest for fame, fortune, and a
place in the sun.

D. H. Lawrence said of *The Scarlet Letter* that it was "so
deep, so dual." So is *My Kinsman, Major Molineux*. That is
why there can be no question of whether Robin made the
right choice. Hawthorne did not want judgments about Robin's rightness or wrongness; he wanted his readers to go
through the pain of Robin's experience so they could understand it and even perhaps understand his own ambivalence
about loyalty and politics.

Hawthorne, in a famous letter to his mother, written in the
spring of 1821 before he was seventeen, said that he wanted
to be an American writer:

> What do you think of my becoming an author, and relying
> for support upon my pen? . . . How proud you would feel
> to see my work praised by the reviewers as equal to the
> proudest products of the Scribbling Sons of John Bull. But
> authors are always poor devils and therefore Satan may take
> them.

To be an American writer, however, required some allegiance to democracy and in that Hawthorne was profoundly ambivalent. That is not to say that he was antidemocratic—he was virtually alone in New England in being a Democrat and supporter of Andrew Jackson—but that he was profoundly unsure of the nature of his allegiance to popular government. The revolution which stirred his imagination to write the story was the on-going American revolution signified by the election of Andrew Jackson in 1828 and his inauguration in March of 1829. Richard Hofstadter writes of that time in words applicable to Hawthorne's story, "The main themes of Jacksonian democracy . . . were militant nationalism and equal access to office." (Country and jobs are what Robin has to learn about.) Despite his frequent and favorable references to Jackson, Hawthorne's real feelings were, I think, both deep and dual. The scion of New England Puritans probably felt that the triumph of Jacksonian democracy was necessary and desirable, but his unconscious mind suggested that the bitter repudiation of John Quincy Adams, fellow citizen of Massachusetts, was a terrible price for that triumph. That part of him could have imagined Jackson as the military figure with the knobbed forehead in Robin's nightmare.

Hawthorne wanted to overthrow the British tyranny in English letters, but he was a most reluctant rebel. In embodying his fantasy in a story, he arranged it so that all of the sympathy of the tale, not the teller, goes with the established order. The mob procession in *My Kinsman, Major Molineux* is an unholy spectacle that seems the combination of an election parade and the orgiastic expression of popular will which marked the inauguration of Andrew Jackson. Hawthorne, disturbed by such expressions of *vox populi,* knew that a prerevolution mob had sacked the house of the same Governor Hutchinson mentioned in the first paragraph of the story and had trampled his manuscript for a history of the colonies. Hawthorne links the French and American revolutions in a story that ostensibly antedates both because he is actually writing about the spirit of revolution in the modern world, a noble spirit that is also destructive of aesthetic and historical values.

Hawthorne writes so feelingly of Robin's ambivalence because it is so close to his own attitude. I think Hawthorne did not republish the story in book form for almost twenty years because he was afraid that he had given away too much to the enemy, that he had exposed too great a gap between the American and the artist. Only in the security of his later years did he put the tale before a wide audience; ironically the greatness of the story was unnoticed for a century until it was taken up by Q. D. Leavis, a scribbling daughter of John Bull.

Hamlet is the first modern political fable and the prince, cursed to remove the impostume from the kingdom, the first modern political protagonist. Francis Fergusson has written of the reciprocal pattern of chaos in the cosmos, chaos in the soul, in that play. The pattern repeats itself in the politics of fiction: how does one arrive at and hold on to a personal system of values when political values are in shambles? The question posed in different ways by *The Republic* and the Nuremberg trials is whether one can be a moral man in an immoral state. Or, as it appears in *Hamlet*, it is the question of authenticity. If one is in opposition to the existing political order, what insures that the individual position is moral? Hamlet's agony is his search for validation, for justification of his private act of vengeance. A sensitive man may know that he marches to a different drummer but must, like Hyacinth Robinson, wonder whether he acts in the name of some higher good or merely to satisfy some personal spite. After all, Joan of Arc may have been a saint of God, or merely a saint of France, or even simply a mad girl, useful to her betters. Our sense of politics from the beginning of the last century to this moment is a sense of organized aggression, confused progress, and the advancement of noble motives for questionable deeds. What the novelists have rendered is the chaos in the souls of men who seek a moral order in a disordered world.

After the opening paragraph of *My Kinsman, Major Molineux* in which the clue to the historical significance of the story is given, Robin journeys on a ferry clearly intended to call to mind Charon, the Styx, and Hades. The story that follows is the story of Robin's experience of certain political realities. The artist was clearly the antenna of the race and perceived what we learned fully only in this century: for modern man the journey into politics can be a journey into hell.

Chapter Three

Dostoyevsky:
The Political Gospel

THE FACT that matters most for Dostoyevsky's life, fiction, and politics is the fact of his resurrection. Only a man who believed he had been judged could write a novel like *The Possessed* in which the political standard is the Last Judgment.

Since we do not often think of the Last Judgment, it is difficult to account for a dramatic response to a novel which demands that we consider active politics as but one step removed from Judgment Day. We in the West have not for some time considered politics as eschatology and the wonder of *The Possessed* is that Dostoyevsky makes us feel that the political arrangements by which we stumble from day to day, from achievement to achievement, from failure to failure, ought to be judged against a religious absolute. While we read the novel, and for some time afterward, we are controlled by the fierceness of Dostoyevsky's conviction: anything less than the absolute is trivial and the trivial will, if unchallenged, become its own absolute. The horror of the novel, in which the reader participates, is that the human acts and the human institutions in a provincial town are judged as they might be by the Creator and most of the characters are vomited out of His mouth.

The road to this eschatological vision began in Petersburg in the spring of 1847 when Dostoyevsky, then a moderately successful young writer, joined the Petrashevsky Circle. This political-intellectual group met for cards and discussions of current events on Friday evenings and included liberals, radicals and at least one police spy. For his activities in this group and specifically for the public reading of a radical letter at one meeting, Dostoyevsky was to spend ten years in exile, four of them in a Siberian labor camp. The experience of prison and exile provided the metaphor of death and rebirth which shapes his fiction; the men and events of 1848 and 1849 provided the models for his great political novel begun twenty years later.

Dostoyevsky came to write *The Possessed* in 1869 when he read a newspaper account of the murder of a student, Ivan Ivanov, by a group of radicals led by one Sergey Nechayev, revolutionist, acquaintance of Bakunin and, apparently, a madman. Dostoyevsky's brother-in-law, a fellow student of Ivanov's and the secret revolutionaries, provided other details for the novelist. But that murder and those characters provided only part of his story. At the time he read of the Nechayev affair, Dostoyevsky was struggling with a novel called "The Life of a Great Sinner." The accounts of the Nechayev group and the story of the sinner fused to provide a special perspective on his own past and produced *The Possessed.*

The Possessed is as much Dostoyevsky's story of his involvement with the Petrashevsky Circle in 1849 as it is of the murder of Ivan Ivanov in 1869; in fact, it is both. Petrashevsky and another more radical acquaintance, Nikolay Speshnev, provided models for Stavrogin and Peter Verkhovensky. Another of that 1849 group, Paul Phillipov, an ardent revolutionary, gave his name to the house in which Shatov and

Kirilov live, Fedka hides, and Kirilov finally kills himself. Dostoyevsky belonged to a radical action cell, a smaller, self-designated group, within the Petrashavesky Circle. Among its accomplishments was the acquisition of a printing press for the secret distribution of radical propaganda. Had the authorities known of this press, Dostoyevsky would almost certainly have been executed. *The Possessed* is a story of two generations, of the radicals of 1849 and the murderers of 1869. Dostoyevsky wrote the novel this way partly because the political murder of a student in the 1860's brought home to him an overwhelming sense of his own political salvation in the 1840's.

But the Nechayev affair belongs to the time after his return to earth. The beginning of the end of Dostoyevsky's first life was his arrest and imprisonment in the Petropavlovsky fortress in Petersburg on April 23, 1849. The charges against him and his associates stemmed from their activities at Petrashevsky's Friday night *levées*. After eight months of investigations and judicial and royal deliberation, a decision for penal servitude was reached and a cruel charade for the prisoners was organized.

On December 22, 1849, Dostoyevsky and twenty other prisoners were taken to Semyonov Square where they heard their death sentences read and saw the firing squads prepare. Dostoyevsky watched as the first group of prisoners was blindfolded and tied to posts. As the rifles were raised, a messenger, as arranged, rode into the square shouting to stop the executions and announced their pardon. Dostoyevsky did not, like one of that first group, go mad on the spot. But that moment of reprieve, that moment of death and resurrection, gave him a special sense of the meaning of his own life and the shaping metaphor for everything that he was to write.

The Possessed is, then, the fusion of newspaper accounts of a radical murder, of personal anecdotes about the murderers and the victim, of faltering attempts at a great confessional novel, and of vivid memories of underground political activities. The energy for that fusion comes from the climactic experience in the snow on Semyonov Square. What *The Possessed* asks us to contemplate is the ultimate consequences of political belief. Dostoyevsky felt that he knew, as did none of his contemporaries, what it meant to consider the final consequences of political belief; that he had, in fact, faced them. From that feeling came the conviction that he was witness to the truth that political salvation lay with messianic nationalism and that he, Fyodor Dostoyevsky, was called to slay the beast of socialist and internationalist error.

The nineteenth century is strangely millennial: history ground on, more or less influenced by new theories which were to end history. Those we remember or know about are mostly the absolutes of the articulate radicals: the political has no right to exist unless it can be proved to be just. Dostoyevsky offered another absolute: real justice is not of this world and reason is the enemy, not the instrument, of a political order. The passion of Dostoyevsky's prose comes from his sense of himself as a true prophet trying to be heard amid the babble of the false prophets. He is also aware, in writing *The Possessed,* that in attacking the enemy he is attacking some old part of himself, some part that his new, resurrected self wants to hate. What holds together the uneven texture of *The Possessed* is the power of Dostoyevsky's vision of political absolutes; he recounts the history of a town which comes to judgment and reveals in that judgment the meaning of politics and the meaning of society.

The Possessed is a prophetic novel because Dostoyevsky thought himself a prophet and because his novel asks us to judge our politics by imagining them before God's judgment on the last day. The novel is both an account of events in the recent past and a chronicle of the future—a description of the possession that will be unless something is done. Thus Dostoyevsky foretells the abomination of desolation that will come upon the unredeemed land and the book could be subtitled "The History and Fate of a Small Provincial Town, Wherein Is Pictured the History and Fate of the Nation, Wherein Is Pictured the End of the World." The prophet would expect his audience to hear the blasphemy in Peter Verkhovensky's statement to Governor von Lembke that he needs only six days in which to complete all his plans.

In a more literal and more frightening sense, the novel is a prophecy. Lieutenant Erkel, loyal follower of the leader of the cell, is so clearly the picture of a man like the Adolf Eichmann we came to know seventy years after the novel was finished that it is impossible to read the description of him without shuddering:

> Erkel was the sort of "little fool" who lacked the real sense that should rule a man's head, but who had plenty of minor, subordinate sense, even to the point of cunning. He was fanatically and childishly devoted to the Movement—that is, essentially to Peter Verkhovensky, on whose instructions he was acting. These instructions had been given him at the meeting of our local Five, when the assignments for the next day were decided on and handed out. Peter Verkhovensky had given Erkel the job of messenger, taking him aside and talking to him privately for ten minutes or so. Carrying out orders was a vital need of Erkel's shallow, unthinking nature, which longed instinctively to be subordinated to another will. Oh, it goes without saying, it could only be in the name of some "great, common cause"—but what cause made no difference. Rank-and-file fanatics of Erkel's type cannot understand the idea they are supposed to serve without fusing it with the person who, in their opinion, expresses it. This sensitive, kind, gentle boy was perhaps the coldest of the killers set on Shatov. He was capable of participating in murder without any personal hatred, without batting an eye.

A cold shiver ran through me when I first read this passage just after the capture and trial of Adolf Eichmann. Such insight makes it impossible to dismiss the bizarre political vision of *The Possessed,* for if Erkel was seen so clearly before, in fact, he really existed, then how much else of the novel has already been realized.

Dostoyevsky begins, not with a political order, but with the soul of man in whatever political order it might inhabit. He said of himself, "I am a realist in a higher sense, that is, I depict the depths of the human soul." The "higher realist" deals with what men are capable of and he creates Erkel, the proto-Nazi, not from special knowledge of totalitarian discipline, but from his knowledge of human potential. Nazism makes men like Erkel effective, but men like Erkel make nazism possible. Erkel needs a leader; he needs to be "possessed." Peter Verkhovensky recognizes that need and puts it to use. Nazism is not a product of the German soul— although that soul may have been more hospitable than others, it is the realization of a human potential for evil: of Erkel's need to have a cause and a leader in which to believe.

One of the best scenes in the novel involves Erkel and Verkhovensky. In the strange economy of the novel, this scene parallels that of Verkhovensky and Stavrogin on the crowded and fatal night in which Peter begs Nikolai to be the savior. The morning scene between Peter and Erkel is almost a burlesque of the drama of the midnight scene of supplication.

The scene to which I refer is section III of Chapter 6 of Part Three, in the railroad station, "at exactly ten minutes to six in the morning," as Peter Verkhovensky prepares to leave the town and the novel, to escape as did his prototype in the murder plot, Sergey Nechayev. Dostoyevsky, who equated punishment with regeneration, in having Verkhovensky escape, is clearly damning him.

Peter is pacing the platform, with the faithful Erkel attending him. By this time we have already had Erkel characterized for us and have witnessed his role in the execution of Shatov. In four pages, however, Dostoyevsky reverses our feelings about Erkel as a human being so that the political thesis is even clearer. It is now the morning after; Shatov has been murdered, Kirilov has committed suicide; the Five has begun to disintegrate badly. Master and follower await the train; Peter pacing boldly and openly, Erkel holding back:

> Erkel seemed eager to have a serious talk during these last minutes, although he himself probably wouldn't have known exactly what about, but he didn't dare say anything because he thought that Peter was tired of him and was waiting impatiently for the final departure signal.

"He thought that Peter was tired of him. . . ." Erkel has been the most loyal and efficient accomplice in the bizarre plot and he is afraid that he is tiresome. This kind of insecurity, which every person in the world has felt at some time, is seen by Dostoyevsky, with his peculiar genius, as one of the roots of totalitarianism: the leader need only control such self-doubt for his own ends.

In the brief dialogue which follows, Peter does exactly that; scolding and cajoling Erkel until he says to him, "But above all, you yourself—never lose courage." Peter speaks here like an earnest father, or a coach, to a bothersome child and Erkel responds with the hopeless love and knowledge of a child, "Ah, I wish you didn't have to leave." Not reassured, he goes on:

> "Mr. Verkhovensky," Erkel said diffidently but firmly, "even if you were actually going to Petersburg, I would still know that you were doing the best thing for the common cause."

Erkel is beyond hope: *"Even if . . . I would still. . . ."* He knows that Peter is running to Petersburg to save his own hide. Erkel allows him to lie and explains the lie in advance. Like Shatov, whom he has just helped to murder, Erkel needs, above all, to believe. It is easier to believe in the devil. Erkel continues to abase himself:

> "Sure, Mr. Verkhovensky, and even if they told me that you were going abroad, I would understand. I realize that you must watch out for your personal safety because you're

everything and we're nothing. I understand that very well."
The poor boy's voice was trembling.

"Thank you, Erkel—ouch!—you touched my sore finger!"
Erkel had awkwardly pressed Peter's hand, forgetting about
the sore finger, which was neatly covered with a black silk
finger sheath.

Suddenly Erkel's obsession is clear: he is a child who wor-
ships Peter and will do anything for him. In his own way
he loves Peter. The details—the trembling voice and the
clumsy touch—force us to sympathy for Erkel's stupidity and
devotion. When, in the Epilogue, the narrator of the events
in the novel tells of Erkel's fate, we understand him completely.

> . . . it is unlikely that any leniency will be shown toward
> Erkel. From the moment of his arrest, Erkel was tight-lipped
> and, if he said anything at all, it was only to try and mislead
> the police. No one has ever heard a word of regret out of him.
> At the same time, however, even the severest investigators
> couldn't help feeling a certain sympathy for him, because of
> his youth and his helplessness and because he was so obvi-
> ously nothing but a young fanatic used by a political manip-
> ulator. Most of all, they were touched by the fact that he
> was sending his mother more than half his scanty army pay.
> His mother is in town now. She's a sick woman, prematurely
> aged. She goes around crying and begging the authorities to
> spare her boy. Whatever one may say, many among us are
> very sorry for Erkel.

To create some sympathy for Erkel is part of Dostoyevsky's intention. But the reader knows more about the cold-
bloodedly murderous activity of this "young fanatic" than
does the narrator, and the twentieth-century reader knows
everything about his descendants, so the sympathy does not
come easy. Yet, it is there.

To go back to that station platform in the early morning,
the statement of Erkel, ". . . you're everything and we're
nothing," is a counterpoint to the scene between Peter and

Stavrogin, when the role of supplicant is Peter's and, combining sex and power, he says: ". . . 'You're just what I need. I don't know anyone like that except you. You are the leader, the sun, and I'm your worm—.' And he suddenly kissed Stavrogin's hand . . . [Stavrogin] pulled his hand away in horror."

The relationship between Peter and Erkel is clearer: leader and follower are linked in the same perversion, the same soullessness. That the town, after the holocaust, does feel sympathy for Erkel and a grudging admiration for Peter— "ah, what an organizer"—is a measure of the degree of corruption in a body politic waiting to be exploited. Mysteries, miracles, authority, according to the Grand Inquisitor, are what mankind really wants.

The scene on the platform ends with Peter abandoning Erkel. It is the nature of such relationships that treason seems inevitable. Peter meets a rich, amusing young man who invites him into "first class" for a game of cards to pass the time on the trip. Erkel helps Peter to move into the first-class carriage and then:

> "Well, Erkel," Peter said hurriedly, shaking Erkel's hand through the carriage window for the last time, "they're waiting for me to start that game."
>
> "You don't have to explain to me, Mr. Verkhovensky; I understand!"
>
> "Well, in that case, I wish you all the best."
>
> And Peter turned away from the window because the young gentleman was calling him, wanting to introduce him to the other two players. And that was the last Erkel saw of his Peter Verkhovensky.
>
> He returned home quite depressed. It wasn't that he was frightened at Peter's leaving him so suddenly but—but Verkhovensky had so readily turned his back on him, as soon as that elegant young man had called to him. Hadn't he really had anything else to say to him, Erkel, besides "all the best?" Couldn't he at least have pressed his hand a bit harder?

Yet in spite of this realization of his jealousy, hurt, sense of loss, and abandonment, Erkel will remain loyal and defy the authorities. Our reactions, so carefully controlled by Dostoyevsky, are similar to those we have to the officer in Kafka's *In the Penal Colony*. In spite of ourselves, as we come to know the officer and Erkel in some human way, we cannot hate them. Our knowledge of them and our feeling for them make more frightening any hatred we feel for the political systems in which they were born to flourish.

What makes Dostoyevsky so alien to Western, liberal, rational, and secular political thinking is the absolutism of his vision. He has no patience with our relativistic, evolutionary, or ameliorative political theories. For him, men will act insofar as they are possessed by an idea, and the only hope for a political order is that men will act as if they were possessed by Christ. Failing that, they will be possessed by devils and destroyed by devils. As the epigraph from Luke and the fates of Stavrogin and Shatov show, only Christ can redeem this time. If not Christ, then the brilliant, frenetic, foppish, perverse, cold, Mephistopheles, Peter Verkhovensky will triumph and take from Kirilov the freedom of his suicide. Thomas Mann, Dostoyevsky's heir, also knew that the modern devil is the devil of cold calculation who offers only the satisfactions of power, manipulation, and isolation.

What makes Dostoyevsky so frightening is the resonance of his prophecy. Caught up in its power, one cannot discuss *The Possessed* as reactionary or obscurantist, or, even more damning, visionary. He renders, as he claimed, the human soul; in this case, that soul in search of a political system in which to validate its own existence. In a character like Erkel, therefore, Dostoyevsky has created the eschatology of totalitarianism: the Last Judgment is here on earth and is rendered by the party. Act accordingly.

Because Dostoyevsky could neither abandon it nor control it, the political thesis is the source of both the power and the problem of the novel. How can an artist make concrete his vision of the *eschaton* as if it is about to happen? He can only indicate the way in which it will take place and risk the inadvertent parody in talking of last things in terms palpably less than those of the *eschaton* itself.

The presentation of a cosmic political thesis in the chronicle of a provincial town is only one dimension of the basic problem; *The Possessed* is really two novels. It began from disparate impulses; one to do a serious novel entitled "The Life of a Great Sinner;" the other to write a political pamphlet satirizing the nihilists. The story of the great sinner survives in Stavrogin's confession and beyond to *The Brothers Karamazov* where, in "The Legend of the Grand Inquisitor," Dostoyevsky continues his struggle with the definition of politics as religion. The pamphlet *contra* the nihilists is the story of the murder of Shatov, based on the Nechayev affair, and its protagonist is Peter Verkhovensky.

In the process of composition, Dostoyevsky fused the stories of Stavrogin, the sinner, and Verkhovensky, the radical assassin, because he came to see them as the same story. Thus, Stavrogin's private vice, the abuse of a child, and his sinful apathy take over the political satire, and Verkhovensky, *fils*, becomes a character beyond parody in his capacity for evil. The stories fused in his mind because Dostoyevsky recognized his private sin in one character and his political transgressions in the other and tried to exorcise both in the novel.

The two stories do not fuse completely, however, and there are problems of focus and tone throughout the novel. Perhaps the confusion is intended. Perhaps more is involved than Dostoyevsky's notorious disinterest in rewriting and he really intended that we should experience the push and pull of conflicting responses which we do feel. The exhaustion with which we end the book comes, whether or not Dostoyevsky intended it, from the struggle of comprehending the political treatise and spiritual tract out of which, miraculously, Dostoyevsky made a great novel.

The tension of this double response, this clash of two impulses is clear in the scene of the birth of the child to Shatov and his wife. Chapter 5 in Part Three, "A Lady Traveler," is unforgettable; but is it deep pathos or black comedy? A religious drama is taking place: Shatov loves his estranged wife with deep Christian concern; the mother's name is Mary; the birth is taking place at the end of a long, harsh journey in a room without proper accommodations; the legal father, who is not the real father, is present; the whole scene takes place on Nativity Street. Yet, for this symbolic acting out of the birth of Christ, the pace is all wrong. It seems almost as if the film of a solemn nativity procession were being run at the wrong speed.

Shatov's death occurs shortly after and is made more horrible by the nativity scene. As his wife comes to term, Shatov, in a way very like Dostoyevsky himself at the birth of his daughter Sonya, rushes to get help. In the moment of blackest comedy, Shatov rouses Lyamshin and tries to sell back to him a revolver to get money for the midwife. Lyamshin is a miser; he knows that Shatov is about to die and is tortured. If he gives Shatov the money, he will not get it back; if he does not, he is afraid he will compromise the murder plan. Shatov's joyous passion is contrasted with the picture of Lyamshin as the tight-fisted Jew of the most vulgar, anti-Semitic burlesque who must finally, in his fear, part with some of his money.

The grotesque comedy of the scene makes the religious symbolism of the birth seem blasphemous. In a sense it is. To grasp a world in which blasphemy is treason, in which a sin against another man is a sin against the true, the religious, meaning of political order is to understand the political intention of the novel. Thus, the ritual murder of Shatov in which the cell is to solidify its existence as a political force is acted out in sequence with the parody of the Nativity. The action is blasphemy and the nihilists are blasphemers because for Dostoyevsky the sin is the same.

Dostoyevsky, the epileptic and former political prisoner, writes most often of bondage, but his theme is freedom. As nihilism is blasphemy, freedom is a religious concept before it is a political one. But freedom is also a theme of history in both Russia and the United States in the last half of the nineteenth century: 1861 was, in both countries, a climactic year in the politics of freedom and bondage. A parallel series of questions—freedom from what or bondage to what; freedom to do what, or slavery requires what—haunts the literature of both nations. Central to the particular work of the Russian convict, exile, and convert is the question: what is true freedom?

The American and French Revolutions had reopened the question of a just political order and in the post-Romantic and post-Napoleonic generations the question had a special urgency. Orthodox political thinking in the West (and here orthodox means secular) sought to answer the question of true freedom by saying that a just political order is one which provides maximum freedom and maximum security for its citizens. Acting as if the terms would never be in conflict, property laws were enacted which protected the owner (his freedom) in exploiting the worker (his security), and this led to the obvious countercharge that "property is theft."

For Dostoyevsky the paradox of freedom and security is not reconcilable in Western terms because those are secular, if not atheistic, terms. The secular orthodoxy of liberal economics and politics is, for him, blasphemy. His furious hatred of such social thinking leads finally to the caricature of the "long-eared" Shigalov, who represents this kind of political thought. Shigalov, addressing the guests assembled for Virginsky's birthday party, says: "I started out with the idea of unrestricted freedom and I have arrived at unrestricted despotism. I must add, however, that any solution of the social problem other than mine is impossible." The "logical" conclusion of Shigalov that ten percent of the population must be masters and the other ninety percent contented slaves represents a secular, absolutist vision of political organization. Dostoyevsky has no quarrel with the absolutist quality of the vision; indeed his belief that Russia will lead the world to salvation has an element of the ten and ninety percent in it. (For some readers Dostoyevsky never seems really to take the step beyond Russian domination to Russian domination as a means to world salvation.) He makes Shigalov a buffoon because Shigalov bases his absolute order on the human and the relative. (Peter Verkhovensky recognizes this, and he believes that the dialectic will continue until ten percent becomes one and he, Verkhovensky, not Shigalov or the group, will rule.) The blasphemy of the secularist, this parody of a social engineer, which occurs in the chapter in which Herzen and Belinsky are mentioned, is one response to the question of freedom and bondage in strictly human terms.

Shigalov, however, later walks away from the actual murder of Shatov, refusing to participate on the grounds that it is a wasted effort. This I take to be Dostoyevsky's acknowledgment of his heretical rather than antithetical relation to the truth. In Dostoyevsky's vision absolute freedom is possible, but only in absolute bondage to God. Freedom is an absolute, not dependent on one's position as despot or slave. True freedom is freedom from sin, liberation from the bondage of vice. Traditional Christian thought has always included this Augustinian notion that freedom begins within the soul. Dostoyevsky says that to be free, one must embrace God because not to embrace God is to embrace something less than Him, something relative, something human, something which cannot ultimately justify itself, and that is to embrace bondage; to become a slave to sense or to self and to accept an illusion in place of freedom. In the passionate dialogues of Stavrogin, Kirilov and Shatov, the real political questions are argued. The discussions about freedom and political organization by Liputin and Shigalov, the prophetic pomposity of "I wanted to inform the meeting about the suffering of the students and about their protest," and the concern for the problems of the midwives reveal what Goethe called "the bondage of the trivial."

The idea that the only true freedom is spiritual freedom and that all political institutions are to be judged accordingly is a strange one in our post-Machiavellian world. It is not, however, completely alien and we know one form of it in the poetry of John Donne, a man who knew the complicated claims of church and state upon a modern conscience. He writes of spiritual freedom in Holy Sonnet X:

> Batter my heart, three person'd God; for, you
> As yet but knocke, breathe, shine, and seeke to mend;
> That I may rise, and stand, o'erthrow mee, and bend
> Your force, to breake, blowe, burn and make me new.
> I, like an usurpt towne, to another due,
> Labour to admit you, but oh, to no end,
> Reason your viceroy in mee, mee should defend,
> But is captiv'd, and proves weake or untrue,
> Yet dearely I love you, and would be lov'd faine,
> But am betroth'd unto your enemie,
> Divorce mee, untie, or breake that knot againe,
> Take mee to you, imprison mee, for I
> Except you enthrall me, never shall be free,
> Nor ever chast, except you ravish mee.

The happy accident of the phrase "like an usurpt towne" underlines the connection between sonnet and novel in their treatment of the theme of freedom and bondage. But Donne's poem belongs to the minority tradition, and more and more since the seventeenth century thoughts about freedom are political and secular, not spiritual. That is why D. H. Lawrence appears as a radical when, in *Studies in Classic American Literature*, he restates the proposition as a personal belief separate from any religious orthodoxy:

> "Henceforth be masterless." Which is all very well, but it isn't freedom. Rather the reverse. A hopeless sort of constraint. It is never freedom till you find something you really *positively want to be*. . . .

Mastery, kingship, fatherhood had their power destroyed at the time of the Renaissance.

And it was precisely at this moment that the great drift over the Atlantic started. What were men drifting away from? The old authority of Europe? Were they breaking the bonds of authority, and escaping to a new more absolute unrestrainedness? Maybe. But there was more to it.

Liberty is all very well, but men cannot live without their masters. There is always a master. And men can either live in glad obedience to the master they believe in, or they live in a frictional opposition to the master they wish to undermine. . . . ORDER. Know that you are responsible to the gods inside you and to the men in whom the gods are manifest. Recognize your superiors and your inferiors, according to the gods. This is the root of all order.

All of these positions, Donne's, Dostoyevsky's and Lawrence's, are not those of the progressive pattern of Western political thought, the pattern which Dostoyevsky despised. He hated the development of the secular state. We, like Turgenev whom Dostoyevsky also hated, think of the secular state as a great modern creation and consider the separation of church and state as specified in the first amendment to the Constitution of the United States a landmark of political evolution. We read, in our history books, of the growth of tolerance by which is meant political accommodation for religious difference. The decline in power of an institutionalized, national church like that in England is interpreted as a concomitant growth in personal liberty. In this political tradition, in which I was raised and to which I still adhere, passionately, freedom is based on the operation of political and judicial institutions which hold religion solely a matter of private practice. The truly free state is the secular state.

Not so in *The Possessed.* The secular state is the state of Julie von Lembke and her charity ball for the needy governesses. In Dostoyevsky's world the secular state can never guarantee freedom, although it can provide comfortable bondage. What we in the West call progress, Dostoyevsky saw as deterioration. Secularism, liberalism and materialism, even more than liberty, equality and fraternity, were, for him, the hallmarks of the modern political order. Dostoyevsky's great paradoxicalist, the Underground Man, rejects them all and everything symbolized by the Crystal Palace is to be hated, not admired. This is not to say that the Underground Man with his diseased liver is Dostoyevsky's spokesman. He is no more a spokesman than any of the other haunted and haunting characters who stalk and glide through the books. The Underground Man derives his power, however, from the same source as the other characters: from their creator's sense that the character's attitude toward himself and his world is one to which he himself is drawn and in which he does, in part, believe. The difference between the author of *The Possessed* and the Underground Man is that while both scorn the marks of bourgeois progress, the author has not made up his mind on the possibility of a human community.

A true community and a just political order are possible if the terms for such a community are understood. A true community is one of men who have been saved and are, therefore, free. The real political order must be first a religious order, and the true political organization would be what a seventeenth-century visionary would have called the community of saints. Dostoyevsky, in common with that earlier band of passionate men, gives his religious vision an historical and geographical dimension: a redeemed Russia, such as that envisioned by Shatov, is the place in which the new political order will be born.

On a gloomy, rainy night, a setting from the pages of a lurid melodrama, Nikolai Stavrogin, holding a mysterious letter, slips out of his house and goes to find Kirilov and Shatov. These will be his second and third meetings during this crowded night. Just before he leaves the house, Peter Verkhovensky cajoles, paws, flatters, and tries to control him as he does the others in the group. Peter does not succeed in making Stavrogin turn to him to become the "leader," but that possibility colors Stavrogin's conversations with Kirilov and Shatov in the middle of the night.

When they meet, Shatov is afraid of Stavrogin because he has slapped and publicly humiliated him. Shatov has bought a gun from Lyamshin to protect himself (the same gun he tries to sell back to get money for the midwife) and so they begin to talk uneasily. Stavrogin has, in fact, come to warn Shatov that he will be killed and that the "Movement"— really only Peter Verkhovensky—will kill both of them. Moved by Stavrogin's concern, Shatov makes his declaration of belief in the world to come, and Part Seven, Chapter 1, in section II is devoted to that declaration.

First he requires that Stavrogin treat him as a human being. Then he speaks of his exile in America and his former relationship to Stavrogin, "There was no conversation between us; there was a teacher *saying* great words and a disciple who had risen from the dead. You're the teacher and I'm the disciple." Exile and resurrection are important attributes in a Dostoyevskian character. Shatov even quotes a line from one of Dostoyevsky's own letters when he shouts at Stavrogin: "Wasn't it you who said that even if it was proved to you mathematically that the Truth was outside Christ, you would prefer to remain with Christ outside the Truth?" Shatov goes on to his statement of purpose: "I'm raising the nation to God. And indeed, has it ever been otherwise? A people forms the body of its god. A nation is a nation only so long as it has its particular god and excludes as irreconcilable all other gods; so long as it believes that with the help of its god it will conquer and destroy all other gods. All great nations have so believed since the beginning of time."

The climax of this confrontation is famous:

> "All right, I'll ask it differently, if you insist," Stavrogin said, looking at him sternly. "I wanted to find out whether or not you yourself believe in God."
> "I believe in Russia and in the Russian Orthodox Church.

. . . I believe in the body of Christ. . . . I believe that His new coming will take place in Russia. . . . I believe—I believe . . ." Shatov mumbled in ecstasy.
"But in God? Do you believe in God?"
"I—I *shall* believe in God."

This passionate doubt is the core of the vision which controls the novel. That vision is both messianic and apocalyptic as Dostoyevsky hovers between Shatov and his exile, resurrection and martydom, and Stavrogin and his exile, despair and suicide. The messianic vision is of a redeemed Russia that will save the world; the apocalyptic, of despair that will destroy the possibility of redemption and bring about the end of the world.

Only after the events of the twentieth century could the full power of Dostoyevsky's vision be appreciated. Albert Camus, for example, adapted *The Possessed* for the stage because he saw the relationship of that vision to our political experience:

> *The Possessed* is one of the four or five works which I value above all others. . . . The creations of Dostoyevsky, we know so well by now, are neither foreign nor absurd. They resemble us, we have the same heart. And if *The Possessed* is a prophetic book, it is so not only because it announces our nihilism, but because it puts us in the midst of those tortured or dead souls, incapable of loving and suffering in their impotence, wishing but unable to believe, those who are the very same souls which inhabit today our society and our spiritual world. . . . It is, therefore, not only a masterpiece of world literature which is, today, produced upon our stage, but a work of this very moment.

In an extended essay on Dostoyevsky appended to the Pléiade edition of his works, Camus again speaks of the impact of Dostoyevsky's "reality" upon the modern consciousness:

> For me, Dostoyevsky is the first writer who, well before

Nietzsche, perceived contemporary nihilism, defined it, predicted its monstrous consequences, and tried to point out the ways to salvation. . . . The man who wrote: "The questions of God and of immortality are the same as the questions of socialism but from another angle," knew that henceforth our civilization would offer salvation for all or for none. But he knew that salvation could not be extended to all, if the pain of one were overlooked. In other words, he did not want a religion which was not socialist, in the largest sense of that word, but he rejected a socialism which was not religious, in the largest sense of that term. In this way he kept alive some hope for a true religion and a true socialism, even though our world seems to make him wrong on both counts. . . . Whether our world dies or is reborn, Dostoyevsky in either case, will be vindicated. That is why he dominates, . . . in spite of and because of his failings, our literature and our history.

To understand for myself how Dostoyevsky made his unique vision of religious socialism and the end of the world dominate our literature and our history, I began to think of it in terms of the political and social movements in Russia and the world with which he struggles in the novel. Dostoyevsky was born within living, vivid memory of Napoleon and, as the creation of Raskolnikov indicates, he was haunted by the possibilities Napoleon represented. (Stavrogin is some part Napoleon as well as some part Byron, some part the radical Speshnev, and some part Dostoyevsky.) The symbolic value of the Napoleonic legend was that the Corsican had shown that it could be done: that one man could change the nature of his own country and then change the order of the world. The legend, the legend Tolstoy hated, lives in Hitler, Mao, Stalin and the host of lesser figures, like Franco and Peron, who have made the twentieth, the century of the dictators. Even the democracies have their strong men, Churchill, de Gaulle and Roosevelt, as champions. The meaning of Napoleon for modern political consciousness has never been calculated, nor is it ever likely to be. One man, born without promise or position, was able to turn all of the instruments of government into extensions of himself.

Peter Verkhovensky knows, however, the value of a symbolic leader, of a man who could, in his fearlessness, transform the world. He wants a "Fairy-Tale Prince."

The chapter with that title comes between the dinner of the radicals to celebrate Virginsky's birthday and the suppressed chapter, "At Tikhon's," or, as it is usually called, "Stavrogin's Confession." The "Fairy-Tale Prince" chapter shows two Stavrogins: one is the leader invented by Peter Verkhovensky because his movement needs a leader and he mistakes Stavrogin's despair for fearlessness. The other is Stavrogin himself, the great sinner, crippled by despair and incapable of repentence and rebirth. Peter struggles to make Stavrogin into the leader he wants:

> "I need you. Without you, I'm a zero, a fly in a glass jar, a bottled thought, a Columbus without America. . . . We shall launch a legend [Verkhovensky is referring to the vanished prince of Russian legend] . . . he exists, but no one has ever seen him. Ah, what a marvelous legend we could let loose on them! The main point is that a new authority is coming and that's just what they'll be longing and crying for. What use can we have for socialism? It destroys the old authority without replacing it. But we will have authority—authority such as the world has never before heard of. All we'll need then will be a lever to lift the earth, and since we have it, we'll lift it.

Stavrogin is specifically an anti-Christ; that is made clear in the chapter following this one with its terrible parody of "Suffer the little children to come unto me." Peter, the devil, acts out the temptation in the wilderness, the temptation to seek dominion on earth. Revealing his own sexual relish for their joint enterprise, Verkhovensky speaks of the institutions of government as if they were extensions of people which can be violated by a man who claims them in the name of a superior dispensation.

Napoleon had found, if only for a moment, the Archimedian point to which Peter refers, and Stavrogin is, as was Raskolnikov, a potential Napoleon. Dostoyevsky himself had been captivated by such a man. He called Nikolay Speshnev, one of the radicals with whom he was associated in 1849, his Mephistopheles, and it was easy for Dostoyevsky to project from his experience the domination by one man of an entire people.

Dostoyevsky is also deeply involved in Peter Verkhovensky's proposition. In the drama of the book it must seem plausible to the characters, and through them the readers, that Peter and Stavrogin together might achieve Peter's proposed conquest of the world. History, in Napoleon and others, offers one kind of substantiation for such a belief. Another comes from the force with which the proposition is presented which moves the reader to entertain the possibility. The power comes from Dostoyevsky's own conviction. Not only was he himself once caught up in a revolutionary act, Peter's attitude is that of the instinctive gambler: he will risk all on a turn, a chance, a person and believe with some part of himself that the gamble will pay off in a way that redresses all the imbalances of the past. Such gambles have worked to make men powerful, but in this novel that gambler's attitude was one of the personal devils Dostoyevsky was exorcising.

The years in which Dostoyevsky associated with the liberal Petrashevsky and the radicals Durov and Speshnev were years in which Europe shivered with the efforts of men to remake the world. In the time of revolutions in France, Germany, Austria and Italy, and of *The Communist Manifesto,* Dostoyevsky thought there was a spectre haunting Europe. After his exile and resurrection, he changed completely his definition of the spectre and embodied it in Peter Verkhovensky. Camus speaks of that change in this way:

> For a long time it seemed that Marx was the real prophet of twentieth century conditions. Now his prophecy seems to

have miscarried. And we are discovering that Dostoyevsky
was the true prophet. He prophesied the reign of the Grand
Inquisitors and the triumph of force over justice.

The experience of Dostoyevsky and the other novelist-
exiles discussed here seems to indicate that one must step
outside the nation-state in order to understand it more fully.
The novelists of politics begin with a sense of the end of the
nation-state. Both senses of "end," purpose and conclusion,
are intended. Dostoyevsky's exile is bounded by *The Communist Manifesto* and *On the Origin of Species,* but during that exile he came to believe in a kingdom not of this
world.

Evolution, progress and triumphant revolution (peaceful
or otherwise) are the driving themes of nineteenth-century
social movements. One of the sacred books of Russian radicalism was Chernyshevsky's *What Is to Be Done* and implicit
in the title of this book, which Dostoyevsky hated, is that
there are answers. Having lived through, in the last century,
what has been done, and shuddering at the thought of what
might be done, we incline more to the perspective of Dostoyevsky's Underground Man and regard the concepts of
evolution and progress more with irony than adoration. Part
of our problem, however, in responding to *The Possessed* is
that we, like Shatov, *want* to believe. We want to believe in
the rational, ordered evolution of the nation-state into a just
and universal political order. Unfortunately, the prophecy of
the reactionary, obscurantist, fanatical, anti-Semitic novelist
comes closer to our actual experience.

Dostoyevsky succeeds in moving us because he is not interested solely in condemning the ideas of evolution and progress. He is interested in demonstrating that what appear in
history as social movements have their origins and their ends
in human aspirations. The concepts of evolution and progress
were neither abstract nor illusory when Dostoyevsky chal-
lenged them. For the nineteenth century, the American and
French Revolutions provided the example that men could

take their political fortunes in hand and remake their world. The revolutions helped to create the idea of the new nation and the new man. The evidence of progress was there before Darwin provided the frame for considering it (despite individual problems) the plan of nature itself. The sense of progress came with the belief that materialism, secularism, and scientism provided almost automatically the freedom, the power, and the energy for making a better political order. The mistake was thinking that the application of power to a problem is a solution. We are now learning what was visible only to the most perceptive authors of the nineteenth century: technology and power speak best to problems of control and domination. The first human problem was to learn to survive as a species; the next human problem is to learn to live with the creations of the species.

Socialism, the catch-all term for the schemes, plans, and theories to improve on tribal organization, has been defined by Bertrand Russell as, "The attempt to conceive imaginatively a better ordering of human society than the destructive and cruel chaos in which mankind has hitherto existed." For Dostoyevsky, however, such an attempt is redeemed only by submission to a divine sanction or it will result, through its pride, in an even more cruel chaos. This is the lesson of the change from Verkhovensky *pere* to Verkhovensky *fils*. Peter realizes that a rational ordering of the world does not provide for miracles, mystery, or authority and that, if he can provide them, he will rule.

The difficulty, as both Dostoyevsky and Bertrand Russell knew, is making the imaginative conception—religious or secular—prevail. In this way it is possible to understand history in dramatic terms. First comes the vision—the conception of a justly ordered state that does not yet exist. The vision separated from power is ideology. Political power is exercised in terms of action and that "action" is the *praxis* of Aristotle's *Poetics* and *Politics*. The action is to make ideology prevail.

One of the great historical dramas of the nineteenth century was the attempt to make ideology prevail. The means varied from democratic reform to national expansion to the terrorism of the right and the left. This "action"—Aristotle's word for that combination of motive and goal, the projection of a potential that is to be made actual, which is peculiarly human—of the making real an idea shaped much of nineteenth- and twentieth-century history.

Dostoyevsky, James, Conrad, Kafka and Mann, the recorders of our historic tragedies, knew that ideology becomes a problem because it leads men to action, and politics and fiction meet over the question of what one does in the name of ideology. To make an ideology prevail is the motive of Bismarck and Bakunin, and those names represent the struggle to create states in which individuals are clearly defined by the ideology of the state itself. Artists saw the dramatic forces at work in politics and created characters who show the consequences of "the will to power." The novelists saw that no ideology would prevail without a battle and that the battle would have human casualties. Dostoyevsky believed that unless the ideology was the idea of Christ in the person of the Russian people, there would be only destruction and despair.

———◆———

While engaged in his two-year struggle with *The Possessed*, Dostoyevsky wrote in a letter to his future biographer Nikolai Strakhov, "Many novels and stories squeeze themselves together into one of my novels, so that there is neither measure nor harmony." Dostoyevsky also said that toward the end of the novel he had to go back and reread the beginning because he had forgotten both the plot and the names of the characters. The danger, then, for the critic is to insist that the work has more unity and structure than it has. Beginning from two different impulses, a political pamphlet and a religious allegory, the book is chaotic and rough-edged. It is, however, a masterpiece; a novel to be taken on its own staggering terms.

Basic among these terms is that of the "return." The theme of return, of coming again to a place, controls the novel. In the most profound sense, the return with which the book is concerned is the return of Christ, the Second Coming which will mark the end of all natural orders. It is as a preparation for that return to earth that Dostoyevsky would have political organizations exist, and that is why at the end of his novel he has Madame Ulitin read to Stepan Verkhovensky from *Revelations*—the *Apocalypse*—the condemnation of the lukewarm. The profound Biblical myth is juxtaposed with the low comedy of the confrontation of Madame Stavrogin and Madame Ulitin, and again Dostoyevsky reveals the doubleness of his vision: a deeply spiritual novel is based on the mores of a provincial town and its author is both Kirilov and Shatov, the mocker and the believer.

There are, obviously, many meanings of "return" in the book. Each of the major characters has been away from the town and returned to it. Stepan Verkhovensky and Madame Stavrogin had ventured to the capital to restore themselves in the liberal social world (Stepan Verkhovensky calls it his "resurrection"). They return poorer and chastened. Shatov and Kirilov have been to America, and, not finding the promised land, they too have returned. Fedka, the killer, has come back to his hometown. Liza Tishin and Maria Lebyadkin, Stavrogin's crippled and demented wife, have come back to town to their violent fates in the homoerotic world of corrupt men and corrupt politics. The central event and subject of the novel is the return to home and family of the prodigal sons, Peter Verkhovensky and Nikolai Stavrogin. Their return is Dostoyevsky's image for his sense of political nihilism: Stavrogin, an anti-Christ, and his Mephistopheles, Peter Verkhovensky, enact a parody of the return of the Son that will bring redemption.

The prodigals return to haunt their parents and that

homely phrase—"come back to haunt you"—captures part of
the ominous tone of the novel and hints at the theme of possession from which Dostoyevsky derived his title. Verkhovensky and Stavrogin (and Fedka) threaten their paired parents
and the whole bourgeois world.

The metaphor of return becomes part of the prophecy of
the novel. Dostoyevsky pillories Turgenev in the character of
Karamazinov and, in fact, is attacking the Westernizer in the
whole concept of the novel, his version of *Fathers and Sons.*
In *The Possessed,* the older generation of liberals, represented by Stepan Verkhovensky, produced the nihilists, and
Nikolai Stavrogin and Peter Verkhovensky are the products
of their parents and teachers. Secular liberalism is corrupt
and will have its own end.

The prodigals in *The Possessed* return, not to repentence,
but to death and destruction and Peter Verkhovensky to an
extraordinary act of parricide. Freud's essay on Dostoyevsky
considers parricide in his life and in *The Brothers Karamazov;*
I want to consider the complicated symbolism of parricide in
The Possessed.

Dostoyevsky's "purpose" in the novel—announced in the
epigraph and the final scene with Stepan Verkhovensky—is
to exorcise the nihilistic devils who are striving for possession
of the Russian soul. But as with almost everything in Dostoyevsky, there is a double purpose; the national exorcism is
matched by a more subtle, more personal one. Dostoyevsky
is exorcising the devils from Russia and from himself.

On April 4, 1866, there was an attempt on the life of Alexander I which upset Dostoyevsky very much. Shortly after his
death, in 1881, his wife remarked that it was well he died
when he did because he would not have survived the assassination of Alexander II one month later. Even more than the
ordinary Russian, Dostoyevsky would react to the killing of
the czar as to an act of parricide. The reformed Dostoyevsky
was genuinely upset by that 1866 attempt, but he must have
had some mixed feelings. The father of Alexander, Czar

Nicholas, had arranged the cruel charade of the mock execution and sent Dostoyevsky to Siberia. (Dostoyevsky could not have known that the czar had actually reduced his sentence even though he approved the fake death scene.) With much deeper feeling, then, he took up Turgenev's model and wrote of fathers and sons.

Yet there was another score to settle, another demon to exorcise. Shortly after his own father was murdered, Dostoyevsky's literary career was launched by the approval of the leading critic of the day, Vissarion Grigorevich Belinsky. Belinsky, ten years Dostoyevsky's senior, praised the manuscript of *Poor Folk* in such terms that Dostoyevsky, like Byron, awoke to find himself famous. More than a literary critic, Belinsky was a leader of progressive, political thought in the 1840's. The friendship of the two men cooled rapidly, however, as Belinsky was less enthusiastic about subsequent works, and they were estranged when Belinsky died shortly before Dostoyevsky's arrest and exile.

Yet, memories lingered and Dostoyevsky projected into Belinsky all that he came to hate in his own political radicalism of the 1840's. Belinsky represented to Dostoyevsky all that he hated in the devoted Westernizers because the novelist had become a convert to his own special brand of Slavophilism. In 1871, while working on *The Possessed,* he wrote to Strakhov calling Belinsky, "the most stupid, shameful and evil-smelling phenomenon in Russian life." The feelings, as he goes on to recount Belinsky's blasphemies in front of him, are very strong about a man dead for more than twenty years. Two years later, in *The Diary of a Writer,* he speaks of his initial warmth and friendship with Belinsky. His biographer, David Magarshack, my source for these statements, attributes the change to Dostoyevsky's changed sense of political security which came with his official connection with the extreme right of the czarist party. This may be true, but other reasons were working.

Dostoyevsky regarded Belinsky as a kind of intellectual

father and he had to be slain as part of Dostoyevsky's progress toward submission to czar and Church. That progress
was never without violence, and Belinsky, even after twenty
years, represented to Dostoyevsky his old, unredeemed self,
the self of socialism, subversion, and atheism. The hated
Turgenev had dedicated *Fathers and Sons* to the memory of
Belinsky. Dostoyevsky had old scores from the 1840's and
settled them in the novel. Part of the violence of the novel,
however, derives from the fact that Dostoyevsky is again
killing his father and himself. The hateful power with which
Peter Verkhovensky destroys his father derives from Dostoyevsky's own feelings, feelings that must be exorcised.

In a very personal sense, then, Dostoyevsky is also "returning" in this book; returning to the man he was before his
resurrection. This is how he talks of that connection in *The
Diary of a Writer:* "How do you know that the Petrashevists
could not have become the Nechayevists, that is, have set
themselves on Nechayev's very path, in such an instance,
were things to have taken a similar turn? Of course, at that
time it was impossible even to imagine how things could
develop and take such a turn. But permit me to speak concerning myself only: probably I could never have become a
Nechayev, but a Nechayevist, this I do not vouch; it is possible, I too could have become one . . . *in the days of my
youth."* In the novel, then, Dostoyevsky must commit parricide and then exorcise that crime. It is as if Dostoyevsky must
place impossible burdens upon his works before he can make
them succeed.

The possessed, the devils of the title, do come to inherit
the earth for a moment. The provincial town of the novel,
from the governing von Lembkes to the outcast Fedka, represents the world. In Dostoyevsky's view, the political fabric
is the sum of redeemed personal relationships, and the point
of the panorama in this novel is to show a world bankrupt at
all levels in all of the recognizable human relationships. Since

the personal relationships have failed, the devils are free to try to destroy the political order. As Steinberg says, "His imagination was permanently fastened on this one and indivisible reality: on a world without stability, in the throes of utter spiritual confusion, exposed to the danger of collective insanity, and yet unaware of the perils ahead." The insanity does, in the novel, spread to include the whole world and to destroy a good part of it. We have lived to see that collective insanity spread over a whole continent. We have lived to experience the novel as prophecy.

The collective insanity we call totalitarianism, and Liputin, the wife-pinching chemist, is a remarkable embodiment of the soul of man in a totalitarian state. That soul is revealed fully in Part Three, when the vicious little gossip has pledged himself to assist in Shatov's murder. The night before the assassination, Liputin clutches the passport he keeps handy and tries to make up his mind to flee. He cannot:

> He had suddenly realized clearly that even if he ran away—and he felt that was the thing to do—he still had to decide whether he was going to flee *before* or *after* Shatov had been taken care of. He felt that there was no strength left in him, that he was now nothing but a crude, unfeeling body, an inert mass moved by a terrifying outside force, and that, although he had his passport ready and could very well run away *from* Shatov (for what could be the hurry otherwise?), that really he was escaping neither *before* Shatov nor *from* Shatov but precisely *after* Shatov, that it had already been decreed, decided and settled.

This is what happens to the *petit bourgeois*, the radical proprietor, when fear and violence become the operative political principles. Liputin, and all of the other characters in the novel, are dignified by being made actors in Dostoyevsky's sacred drama of history.

The story of *The Possessed* is strangely like a Gospel. We are told what happened by an eyewitness who indicates that his narrative of strange events and mysterious people has significance beyond his poor powers to relate. There is an uncanny feeling in reading of the events in the novel such as might have overcome a cultivated Roman of the time of Tiberius Caesar at the narrative of strange events in an uncouth, eastern province; events and agitations which disturbed the provincial administration. Those earlier events in the distant province altered the course of history.

The anti-Gospel is the form Dostoyevsky uses for his apocalyptic novel, and at the center of this anti-Gospel is the anti-Christ: Nikolai Stavrogin. He is tempted by Peter, like Christ in the wilderness; Kirilov and Shatov die like the two thieves on either side of him, and Liza Tishin, after her terrible night with him, is killed by a mob in an awful parody of the story of the woman taken in adultery. Stavrogin's Confession, seemingly a product of Dostoyevsky's haunted sense of terrible sin, is the anti-Gospel version of suffer the little children to come unto me and woe to him who scandalizes the child. As Mochulsky says of him, "Stavrogin enters the world of the novel, like a living corpse, hoping for resurrection and not believing in its possibility."

Dostoyevsky came to write this anti-Gospel because it was the only adequate frame for his story. "The Life of a Great Sinner" and an antinihilist pamphlet became one novel because Dostoyevsky came to see, in his own biography, the relation of politics and religion. The story of Stepan Verkhovensky's encounter with Madame Ulitin is based on Dostoyevsky's meeting with Madame Fonvizin at Tobolsk in 1849 when she gave him the copy of the New Testament which he carried on his pilgrimage of resurrection. He also came to feel, as he wrote his novel of the generations, of the legacy of the aetheists of the 1840's to the assassins of the 1860's, his own miraculous salvation: "Probably I could never have become a Nechayev, but a Nechayevist . . . it is possible, I too could have become one. . . ." Like all the characters in his novel, Dostoyevsky had gone away and returned.

He hoped that his experience would enable him to destroy the false prophets who threatened the salvation of Russia.

———◆———

The narrative of present events in *The Possessed* is introduced by two stories from the past. Stavrogin, in his previous sojourn in the town, acted like a madman, biting ears and pulling noses. He goes away and returns only to bring pain and death. His path is out of Russia to suicide. Stepan Verkhovensky, in the retrospect at the beginning, sees his resurrection in a journey to the city to edit a journal for the radicals. He lives to see another kind of resurrection in a mad pilgrimage to the country to give Bibles to the peasants. Neither is saved, but the fool of God in the heart of Russia is closer to Dostoyevsky's ideal of a good citizen.

Stavrogin dies by his own hand, stripped of his Russianness, a citizen of the canton of Uri, an exile from the holy soil from which his creator hoped a new theocracy would spring. That hope was expressed as follows in a letter to Maikov:

> The facts have shown us that the malady which has afflicted civilized Russians was much stronger than we ourselves imagined, and that the affair did not end with Belinsky, Krayevsky, etc. But here we have what the Evangelist Luke bears witness to. Exactly the same thing has taken place among us. The devils went out of the Russian man and entered into a herd of swine, i.e., into the Nechayevs and Servo-Solovyeviches and others. These have drowned or will drown surely, and the healed man, from whom the devils went out, is seated at the feet of Jesus. So it must have been. Russia has vomited up this filth which poisoned her, and now, of course, in those scoundrels who were vomited up there has remained nothing Russian. But observe, my dear friend: he who loses his people and nationality loses also the faith of his fathers and God. . . . And another strength may be our own

faith in our personality, in the holiness of our vocation. The whole vocation of Russia is contained in Orthodoxy, in the *light from the East,* which will stream to mankind who is blinded in the West, having lost Christ. . . . Well, if you want to know, this is precisely the theme of my novel. *It is called The Devils [The Possessed].*

The overwhelming power of the novel does not come, however, from this conscious motive. Rather, it comes from Dostoyevsky's doubt and pain about his own salvation, from his memories of and identifications with the satanic characters in the book, from his own profound ambivalence about parricide, Deicide, and all forms of human violence. Only those tortured feelings could have produced a book so prophetic of modern politics.

In the sardonic opening of the book we meet the pitiful Virginsky and his "bright hopes." He is modeled, in part, on Nikolai Chernyshevsky, the author of *What Is to Be Done,* a convict, exile, and radical hero of the 1860's. (Chernyshevsky is alleged to have said to his wife on discovering that she was unfaithful, "Before this I only loved you; now I respect you.") Even when Virginsky's wife has been unfaithful and he is distraught, he remains a faithful member of the liberal circle in town. Only once does he admit his misery, but he adds immediately, "Ah, it's nothing but a private matter that can in no way interfere with the common cause." Politics and fiction meet in this pitiful statement of the abstract cause as the cure for personal hurt. The conflict of private concerns and common causes is the source of tragedy, and the peculiar tragedy of political fiction is the failure of the political order to bring about its promised end: the fulfillment of private desires in a public order recognized as just, humane, and free.

In 1956 Alberto Moravia published an essay on Dostoyevsky as a political artist entitled, "The Marx-Dostoyevsky Duel." His thesis, brilliantly argued, is that both Marx and Dostoyevsky attacked the existing social order but that they differed in their definitions of evil. For the Marxist, evil is usury and the economic oppression of the capitalist system. For Dostoyevsky, evil is any violence, even violence done to the oppressor. "So," Moravia says, "for the last ninety years, we have witnessed in Russia a kind of match between Dostoyevsky and Marx. The first round was won by Dostoyevsky, since he had written a masterpiece (*Crime and Punishment*); the second round went to Marx, since his theories produced a revolution; yet the third round seems to have been won by Dostoyevsky: the evil thrown out the window by Marxism has returned in torrents through the door of Stalinism, that is, through the means adopted by the revolution to establish and maintain itself."

Fascinated by violence, Dostoyevsky saw for Russia and the world that revolutionary violence will save no one and only the violence of the kingdom of Heaven works. In his vision, politics is a matter of salvation and citizens must declare their allegiance to the party of Christ or the party of Satan. In his fierce political gospel, these are the contending forces. The lukewarm will be destroyed in the struggle.

Chapter Four

James: The Aesthetics
of Politics

AN ENTRY in Alice James' *Diary* for December 1, 1889, could serve as an epigraph for *The Princess Casamassima*. She says, apparently in reference to a newspaper report:

> In a fine speech by John Morley at the Eighty Club, he says that to him—"A working-man who cannot get work is an infinitely more tragic figure than any Hamlet or any Oedipus." Beautifully and nobly said, *Honest John!*

Alice James adds:

> Think of the hideous despair of seeing y[our]self and children sinking into that black, seething, bottomless gulf which yawns before them from the cradle to the grave.

Henry James did not share his sister's certainty about the relative tragedy of Hamlet dead or of Grugan, Roker, and Hotchkin, Hyacinth Robinson's fellow bookbinders, unemployed. In fact, the whole question of *The Princess Casamassima* is the precise relationship of the aesthetic to the economic, political, and moral aspects of human experience. Henry James has no answers to the questions he raises, and his novel ends with the suicide of his protagonist because neither creator nor character can see any way out of the clash of values in the novel.

The Princess Casamassima is a novel of clear vision but mixed motives on the part of both the novelist and his characters. James wanted to write a book in the naturalistic manner on a topic of current concern. He visited Millbank prison, observed, took notes, and prepared himself for a fictional journey into the London underworld. He was fated by his own talent, however, never to have the popular success he so ambiguously courted. Hyacinth Robinson's ambivalence reflects that of his creator, caught between a realistic panorama in the manner of Dickens, Balzac, and Zola and the exploration of a sensitive consciousness in a manner distinctly Jamesian. Neither Hyacinth nor James can give himself completely to the masses. On the other hand, both saw the sham and injustice of an indifferent aristocracy. Creator and character stood between and watched as the "haves" and the "have nots" closed upon each other.

Despite the failure of popular success which hurt James deeply, he does achieve in *The Princess Casamassima* a remarkable group portrait of consciousness in and around a political movement. The political novel is constructed, in my brief definition, upon the study of moral choices among political alternatives. James is concerned to show the origins and consequences of these choices. He does not, however, try to render them in all possible dimensions. He focuses on a theme, the value of aesthetic experience, and uses that as a structural principle in his portrait of a world and its people rushing headlong to Armaggedon.

The aesthetic is not a trivial consideration. If it were, John Morley's proposition would be meaningless. The question is whether the imaginary Hamlet, fat and out of breath, is worth more than a lean, hungry and inarticulate workman grumbling in a real *Sun and Moon*. The radical proposition at the core of *The Princess Casamassima* is that aristocracy is finished, and democracy will not do.

That proposition is not nearly so reactionary as it sounds.

It might, alternatively, be phrased: mere ballot democracy is not enough to replace the aristocratic tradition of government mortally wounded in 1789 and, in 1886, moving clearly to its final resting places in the fields of Flanders and Gallipoli and Tannenberg and the Somme. The fact of the franchise is not enough for James if the state in which the franchise is exercised is not redeemed by some moral idea. That is Matthew Arnold's sense of culture. *The Princess Casamassima* is a great political novel because in it James deals directly with the basic political questions: who are the natural leaders and how are they to be chosen; what is an idea that justifies action; what is the relative value of individual experience to group welfare; what is to be destroyed and what preserved in the name of progress and who is to decide?

Echoing like a musical phrase, the question, *"How far do you go?"* appears more than a dozen times in the book. In telling the story of Hyacinth Robinson, James chose that question carefully. Hyacinth must find his place in his world and the question of limit—"How far, in fact, do you go"—is both aesthetic and moral. Hyacinth's suicide is his answer to the basic question of the novel.

James and Dostoyevsky are usually contrasted, not connected, yet *The Princess Casamassima* and *The Possessed*, published within fifteen years of each other, share a concern for the proper role of the aesthetic in a political order. Hyacinth Robinson is a bookbinder, an artisan who understands his art. His occupation represents his status: in touch with the world of intellect and leisure but not a part of it. (The Princess employs him as her private bookbinder as she might a chaplain or a hairdresser.) Dostoyevsky had the same sense of that craft as had James. In *The Possessed*, when Mary returns to Shatov to bear Stavrogin's child, she speaks to him of her plans:

> "Listen, Shatov, I plan to open a bookbinding shop here based on fair, cooperative principles. Since you live here, what do you think—could it succeed?"

"Ah, Mary, they don't read much in this town. Besides there are hardly any books around. And even if they got hold of a book, why should they have it bound all of a sudden?"

"Who's 'they'?"

"The local readers—the inhabitants of the town in general."

"Well, express yourself clearly. How can I know who you mean by *they?* Can't you learn to talk properly?"

"It's the spirit of the language," Shatov mumbled.

"Ah, go to hell with your spirit; I'm tired of you. Now why shouldn't the local reader or inhabitant have his books bound?"

"Because reading books and having them bound are two different stages in cultural development, two strikingly distinct phases. At first, little by little, man acquires the reading habit. He does so very, very slowly. It may take centuries, and during that time, he throws his books around and tears them, refusing to grant them the status of a serious object. Now, binding a book is a sign that the book is respected, that man not only enjoys reading but now considers the book as a serious object. Well, Russia as a whole hasn't yet reached that second stage, but in Europe they've been binding books for a long time."

Shatov is, as Mary remarks, "rather pedantic," but she adds, he used to be "quite witty."

More is involved in linking the novels, however, than the coincidence of bookbinding in each. They are both concerned with anarchists and anarchism and each book posits a culture, separate from the political order, against which the anarchists rage. The justice of the anarchists and the blindness of the order are conceded. The problem is how to incorporate the culture into the old order and thereby revivify it, or into the new and thereby humanize it. Voting is not enough; the quality of life is at stake.

James and Dostoyevsky are as clear as John Morley in their statement of the tragic alternatives of culture and anarchy. In *The Princess Casamassima,* they are stated in Chapter Thirty. Hyacinth has received his "inheritance" and gone on his grand tour. Hyacinth here seems more and more like

Keats, a young artist frustrated by the knowledge that he will
not live to experience all of the life of which he is capable:
". . . and as he lingered before crossing the Seine a sudden
sense overtook him, making his heart falter to anguish—a
sense of everything that might hold one to the world, of the
sweetness of not dying, the fascination of great cities, the
charm of travel and discovery, the generosity of admiration."
Even though he has mortgaged his life to the cause with his
pledge to act as directed, new experiences begin to alter him.
From Venice he writes to the Princess of his changed feelings:

> Dear Princess, there are things I shall be too sorry to see
> you touch, even you with your hands divine; and—shall I tell
> you *le fond de ma pensée*, as you used to say?—I feel myself
> capable of fighting for them. You can't call me a traitor, for
> you know the obligation I supremely, I immutably recognise.
> The monuments and treasures of art, the great palaces and
> properties, the conquests of learning and taste, the general
> fabric of civilization as we know it, based if you will upon
> all the despotisms, the cruelties, the exclusions, the monopo-
> lies and the rapacities of the past, but thanks to which, all the
> same, the world is less of a 'bloody sell' and life more of a
> lark—our friend Hoffendahl seems to me to hold them too
> cheap and to wish to substitute for them something in which
> I can't somehow believe as I do in things with which the
> yearnings and the tears of generations have been mixed. You
> know how extraordinary I think our Hoffendahl—to speak
> only of him; but if there's one thing that's more clear about
> him than another, it's that he wouldn't have the least feeling
> for this incomparable, abominable old Venice. *He would cut
> up the ceilings of the Veronese into strips, so that every one
> might have a little piece* [italics added]. I don't want every
> one to have a little piece of anything and I've a great horror
> of that kind of invidious jealousy which is at the bottom of
> the idea of a redistribution. You'll say I talk of it all at my
> ease while in a delicious capital I smoke cigarettes on a
> magenta divan; and I give you leave to scoff at me if it turns

out that when I come back to London without a penny in my pocket I don't hold the same language. I don't know what it comes from, but during the last three months there has crept over me a deep distrust of that same grudging attitude—the intolerance of positions and fortunes that are higher and brighter than one's own; a fear, moreover, that I may in the past have been actuated by such motives, and a devout hope that if I'm to pass away while I'm yet young it may not be with that odious stain upon my soul.

The passage is central to the novel and to modern political experience. The question Hyacinth raises is that of loyalty and treason. He can be loyal to Hoffendahl, the mysterious leader of the party to whom he has pledged his life, and to the idea of the new world that he represents; or, he can be loyal to the old world of art. He can choose a private morality of contemplation or a public morality of action. He cannot conceive of combining them.

Dostoyevsky deals with the relation of art to progressive politics early in *The Possessed*, when Stepan Verkhovensky and Madame Stavrogin go to Petersburg and establish a literary and social circle for a group of dubious young activists. The bright hopes of the enlightened couple come to a bad end:

Remaining in Petersburg any longer was, of course, unthinkable. Besides, Mr. Verkhovensky finally proved a complete failure. He couldn't restrain himself and started defending the rights of art. They laughed at him louder than ever. At the final gathering, he decided to touch them with his revolutionary eloquence, hoping to reach their hearts, figuring to gain their sympathy by mentioning his years "in exile." He accepted unquestioningly the uselessness, the ridiculous connotation of the notion "mother country"; he endorsed the theory that religion was harmful; but he declared loudly and proudly that he placed Pushkin's poems above shoes—very much so. They booed him so mercilessly that he dissolved into tears right there on the stage. Mrs. Stavrogin took him home more dead than alive.

Neither Hyacinth Robinson in his letter nor Stepan Verkhovensky in his speech is a spokesman for his creator and the
statements must be read in their dramatic contexts. Their
common theme, however, is the discontinuity of aesthetics
and social justice. Or, as Karamazinov, the poet-pimp, ob-
serves during the disastrous fete: "But I assure you, ladies
and gentlemen, that I have become so realistic in my outlook
that I feel laurels would be more useful in the hands of a
skillful cook than on my head." "Yes, and we have more use
for cooks!" is the answer he receives from a radical student in
the audience.

In the novels of James and Dostoyevsky we watch the
struggle of the artist to define the relationships of the aesthetic and the political in the process of creating an aesthetic form which is meant to represent political substance.
The relationships are defined by contrast: Hoffendahl and
the Veronese ceiling; Pushkin and shoes; poets and cooks.
The implication is that the characters must choose between
beauty and justice. Art is not made, however, from such stark
polarities. Literary art derives its power to stun, to move,
and to haunt us from its ability to show the identities within
the contradictions, the yes-in-no and no-in-yes, which is human experience. Hyacinth Robinson faces a tragic dilemma
of belief and response, of conviction and feeling. Dostoyevsky
makes the attack on the beautiful a weapon for his attack
upon the anarchists. James, usually considered the aesthete,
marks out for himself a more complicated part of this problem and in *The Princess Casamassima* he succeeds in making
the aesthetic a part of his sense of the relation of the political
and the moral.

In the West, since the Greeks, aesthetics and politics have
had a complicated relationship. Periclean Athens is still a
model for beautiful politics and the Roman Empire is judged
at least partially in terms of Vergil's vision of it. We admire
Versailles, if not the kings who built it, and even the Bol-
sheviks made of the Winter Palace a museum. We still judge

a political order by its artistic creations and use aesthetic norms in judging the value of a society. Obviously, time solves many problems and it is easy to value the historical temple divorced from its political reality. That easy course is not open to the novelist who creates a character sweating as he wrestles with his sense of what has been achieved and should be conserved, and his conviction that the price of that conservation is no longer tolerable.

The novel itself is an aesthetic evaluation and *The Princess Casamassima*, like the other works discussed, is a "rendering" of a social and political order that evokes and conditions a response from the reader. In this the novelist is like the pamphleteer. The essential difference between the two is that the novelist does not try to move us to action, but to a new understanding of the tragic complexity of the human condition. By evoking scorn or sympathy, the novelist involves us in comparative judgments of the value of political ideals and professions. A political novel makes the reader a participant in the revolutionary struggle described by Carlyle as that "of disimprisoned Anarchy against corrupt worn-out Authority" with the disadvantage of understanding the virtues of both evils. In the history of the political novel, Dostoyevsky flaunted this idea, Mann was tortured by it, but James made it the subject of his novel.

The Portrait of a Lady opens on a beautiful lawn as the shadows begin to lengthen at the end of a summer afternoon. In *The Princess Casamassima*, the shadows, on the mean streets of London, have grown very long and will soon engulf that other idyllic world of tea and splendor. James is the historian of the end of a century and the end of a world. Most historical epochs can be characterized by some Manichaean duality, or by an Hegelian pattern of clash and conflict, or some vision of losers and winners in a struggle to prevail. The period from 1871 to 1914, called in some history books "the era of the armed peace," is not different. The tension in the period was visible to some of those in it: an age of progress, reform and the beginning of widespread prosperity; an era of violence erupting sporadically until the seams would hold no longer and the guns began to roar all over the world. *Culture and Anarchy* was published in 1869, on the eve of the era in which *The Princess Casamassima* is set. Arnold defined the struggle which led to the violence that is the history of our century: if a nation-state is not infused with the principles of culture as a moral force, then it will succumb to anarchy. Political democracy and material prosperity, good in themselves, are not enough to balance the lusts for power in the darker parts of the heart. The ominous aspects of the later reaches of the gilded age are part of the subject of *The Princess Casamassima.* James recognized the forces that were gathering and knew they would bring not only war, as bad as that would be, but the end of a civilization. When Hyacinth Robinson sprang from the London pavement before his creator, he was an orphan of uncertain national heritage, but he was a leading citizen in the state of modern political consciousness.

In that gilded age, politics was clearly power and to act politically meant to exercise power to make ideology prevail. The most reactionary militarist and the meanest anarchist had some power at hand and were determined to use it in the name of preserving or establishing the proper order. Each of the major powers, as it stumbled toward the war, thought that it could exercise power and that such an exercise, if successful, was its own justification. In *The Princess Casamassima,* James' characters represent all the classes and all the political beliefs of his world, but they also represent the nations of Europe, French, English and German, in the period 1871 to 1914, and the tensions of that world are represented in the stories which make up the novel. Hawthorne embodied the story of his country in the experiences of a boy; James makes the story of Hyacinth represent a world.

Ezra Pound was the first to recognize James' historical significance—who else but another American exile tortured by his own sense of the demands for aesthetic and national loyalty. He wrote of James' concentration on individual freedom and national identity in the long twilight before August 1914.

> I am tired of hearing pettiness talked about Henry James' style. The subject has been discussed enough in all conscience, along with the minor James. Yet I have heard no word of the major James, of the hater of tyranny; book after early book against oppression, the domination of modern life; not worked out in the diagrams of Greek tragedy, not labeled "epos" or "Aeschylus." The outbursts in *The Tragic Muse*, the whole of *The Turn of the Screw*, human liberty, personal liberty, the rights of the individual against all sorts of intangible bondage.

Pound, after saying that he does not think that James was in any way "political," goes on to discuss the prophetic quality of the fiction:

> As Armageddon has only too clearly shown, national qualities are the great gods of the present and Henry James spent himself from the beginning in an analysis of these potent chemicals; trying to determine from the given microscopic slide the nature of the Frenchness, Englishness, Germanness, Americanness, which chemicals too little regarded, have in our time exploded for want of watching. They are the permanent and fundamental hostilities and incompatibles. We may rest our claim for his greatness in the magnitude of his protagonists, in the magnitude of the forces he analyzed and portrayed. This is not the bare matter of a number of titled people, a few duchesses and a few butlers.
>
> Whatever Flaubert may have said about his *Education sentimentale* as a potential preventive of the debacle of 1870, *if people had* read it, and whatever Gautier's friend may have said about *Emaux et Camées* as the last resistance to the Prussians, from Dr. Rudolph Staub's paragraph in *The Bundle of Letters* to the last and almost only public act of his life, James displayed a steady perception and a steady consideration of the qualities of different Western races, whose consequences none of us can escape.

Hyacinth Robinson was, according to his creator, a product of the streets of London: "I arrived so at the history of little Hyacinth Robinson—he sprang up for me out of the London pavement." (James' Preface) London was for James what it was for Conrad a decade later; the center of trade, of empire, of civilization. To the American expatriate and to the Polish emigré, London was the capital of a country and an era. Hyacinth Robinson, as Henry James did, wanders the streets of that city and through him we meet the people at this center of power and empire. We come also to know the city itself—the metropolis that is the symbol of the modern state. This is the city that Conrad will use in *The Secret Agent* to represent the wasteland over which modern man rules. We know in reading *The Princess Casamassima* that it is in this city, and others like it, that modern man has come to his political consciousness; and, however much we admire Levin's pastoral utopianism, it is Raskolnikov's urban grotesque that stands for our world. The substance of *The Princess Casamassima* is the standard stuff of all of James' novels, "social relations." James reminds us that social relations are also moral relations; and in this instance, in the shabby houses and on the gloomy streets of the great metropolis, Hyacinth Robinson learns the extent to which social and moral relations are determined by political arrangements.

But James does not deal in the cosmic politics of Dostoyevsky, nor does he write the sustained allegory of Mann. James, in *The Princess Casamassima,* wrote, with some hope for popular success, in the mainstream of the realistic novel. He shows a "young man from the provinces" searching out his earthly salvation with diligence. The quoted phrase is from Lionel Trilling's justly famous essay on the novel. James, as Trilling says, does more than simply portray that search for a place in the "real" world to which youth aspires. What James does in *The Princess Casamassima* is to show how

political awareness is part of the private drama of consciousness on which he based the novel.

In *The Princess Casamassima*, Hyacinth is taught that sex
and money, guilt and retribution, intelligence and taste, are
political matters. He learns from M. Poupin both bookbinding and radical republicanism. He learns from Mr. Vetch a
socialist ethic. He learns from Pinnie that he has been de-
nied the privileges of the privileged class.

Hyacinth's legacy is his "radicalism." Produced by the
world of privilege and then excluded from it, Hyacinth is a
representative of all the *déclassés* of Europe in the *Belle
Epoque*. All of the moral relations of the book begin with
Hyacinth's sense of himself as an outcast and his vow to do
something about it. Hyacinth, like Robin Molineux, is a
young man who walks through an exotic city testing his
assumptions about his place in the world. In *The Princess
Casamassima*, political beliefs, political attitudes, political
ideology are represented in terms of the morality of interper-
sonal relationships. James is careful in this novel to set those
relationships in a palpable historical world.

The symbol of this world, at the very center of *The Princess Casamassima*, is the house, Medley. We are thrust into
that house and see it, as if through a movie camera held behind Hyacinth's right shoulder, in the opening paragraph of
Chapter Twenty-two, immediately following the fateful meeting with Hoffendahl. We do not know at first how the ride in
the cab through the dark streets of London has ended in this
stately mansion. James wanted in his reader the confusion
produced by the juxtaposition, because the world of which
he wrote is the world of contrast between the interior of *The
Sun and The Moon* tavern, packed with noisy, banal, and
poor people, and the chaste and quiet library at Medley. Both
exist for us in Hyacinth's mind; his intimate knowledge of
both becomes finally more than he can bear. But they were
real places in the real world. James is troubled by the question of the relation of the lawns of Medley to the mean

streets of London, by the ways in which they were connected, and by whether any world could sustain both simultaneously. He puts the two worlds together in Hyacinth's
mind to represent the poles of value in the novel. The dwelling place becomes the symbol: Lomax Place (the "Plice"),
Lisson Grove, Audley Court, Madeira Crescent; where one
lives is how one lives. It is not necessary to trace the biographical dimension of this question for James himself, nor
its antecedent in *Bleak House*. What matters is what James
made of his reading and of his doubt: a novel in which the
house, the dwelling, becomes a symbol of the prize for which
his protagonist strives.

That prize is an authentic life. The quizzical Hyacinth,
who James says in the Preface, had, like a child, always to
know the whole truth, tries to authenticate his own life. That
task, as Gödel would have pointed out, is impossible. So, as
in all the great novels of James, the question is that of the
quality of the impossible guest. Hyacinth, knowing he is
illegitimate and troubled by what he thinks of as his divided
heritage, seeks to make himself legitimate in his own eyes.
That process involves a series of journeys and the one at the
center of the book is to Medley.

The most important fact about Medley is that it is rented.
Medley stands for the best in that world of splendor and
squalor that was Europe before the great war, and the values
in the climactic middle scene are vested in the house and not
the occupants. The owners are absent and there is a feeling
of long, even permanent, absence, of total neglect of the
house. It is available to the Princess for a short term when
Hyacinth visits her there and sees and understands another
world. The owners either cannot afford the house, or are too
busy elsewhere to attend to it. I do not know what happened
to Medley at the end of the book, but I do know what happened to it in 1914. It was part of the "two gross of broken
statues" and the "few thousand battered books" for which,
as Pound said, "there died a myriad,/ And of the best, among
them." Despite the sacrifice, it was not redeemed.

William Butler Yeats cared, as did James, for the civilizing values of great houses. In his essay on *The Princess Casamassima* to which I have already referred, Lionel Trilling says that Yeats' poem "Ancestral Houses" is a companion work to the novel. I would substitute another, lesser known, Yeats poem for that designation:

Upon a House Shaken by the Land Agitation

How should the world be luckier if this house,
Where passion and precision have been one
Time out of mind, became too ruinous
To breed the lidless eye that loves the sun?
And the sweet laughing eagle thoughts that grow
Where wings have memory of wings, and all
That comes of the best knit to the best? Although
Mean roof-trees were the sturdier for its fall,
How should their luck run high enough to reach
The gifts that govern men, and after these
To gradual Time's last gift, a written speech
Wrought of high laughter, loveliness and ease?

Hyacinth is more involved in this kind of struggle than Yeats. He knows more of the "mean roof-trees" than does the poet. He is also committed to the politics of "land agitation." (The novel, in fact, tried to cash in on popular fear of Irish terrorism in the 1880's.) The poem ends in a question to which Hyacinth can find no satisfactory answer.

James, interestingly enough, seems to have felt that Medley was not a sufficient symbol for the conflict he envisioned in his novel. Perhaps he felt he needed something more dramatic. In any case, after Medley, Hyacinth does receive his "inheritance" and, like a young nobleman, uses it to make the grand tour. This completes the contrast of worlds begun by Hyacinth's dark journey to meet Hoffendahl. While on his grand tour, Hyacinth sees a different world and writes to the

Princess of values that are not political or economic. His letter from Venice, the counterpart of the Yeats poem, states his
new sense of himself and his world and says, at the same
time, that he is not a "traitor" to what he knows is right. His
tragedy is that he cannot reconcile in his life the contradictions in his values. The tragedy of his world was that it could
not reconcile the contradiction of Hoffendahl and Medley
given to us in the novel on succeeding pages.

The rented house at the center of the book is up for grabs
and, in that state, is a more potent symbol than it would be
were it clearly the possession of a ruling class. The conflicts
in the novel are not between the decadent rich and the
virtuous poor, or the refined aristocracy and the crude proletariat. There is Medley and what it represents. It is available
to Christina, but she cannot keep it. It is not available to
Hyacinth or Paul Muniment, and it is not clear that they
would know what to do with it. Lady Aurora would be
ashamed or embarrassed to possess it. The house remains,
then, waiting for an occupant, looked after by the Marchants.
We know, from the emotional logic of the novel, that these
pretenders should be displaced by a land agitation. What is
not clear is whether there are legitimate heirs to the house of
culture and privilege. Who is to have the prize in the struggle
of "disimprisoned Anarchy against corrupt worn-out Authority?"

———◆———

Politics is the sum of relationships in a state. James, as well
as Socrates, knew that only moral relationships constituted
a just state. He knew also that the state had to define itself in
such a way that individual moral relationships were possible.
That is partially why James left an America he felt had
chosen to be willfully naive. He discovered that England,
supposedly the nation of the civilized West at its judicial

best, offered no clear pattern of politics and morality. Rather, it produced Millicent Henning; but her form of social Darwinism could not constitute an authentic principle of social organization. *The Princess Casamassima* poses ethical questions, because to James' very classical mind, politics is defined by ethics. It is also, to his artistic mind, defined by aesthetics. What he has done, stated simply, is to write a novel in which aesthetics and ethics, art and politics, are the terms of the struggle in the mind of his protagonist. Since, in the novel and, by implication, in the world, they cannot be reconciled and since no justification for the individual is possible until they are, the tragedy is inevitable.

I think that is the sense in which James speaks of Hyacinth in the Preface, as a little bookbinder on whom nothing is lost. The Princess, absolutely fascinating and absolutely devoid of moral sense, is as aware of the aesthetics of politics as a Byzantine empress. Paul Muniment seems an honorable and intelligent man, yet he has no taste. Even to his fine mind, the crudest bourgeois comforts of Madeira Crescent are something to be wondered at. These characters survive because only certain experiences are available to them and they are consistent in those experiences.

James decides for the ethical over the aesthetic in the resolution of his novel. He could not have done otherwise. A paradox of literary art is that it must be devoted totally to aesthetic ends but must never present them as superior to ethical concerns. T. S. Eliot pointed to this when he said that only on aesthetic grounds could we determine whether something was literature; but only on nonaesthetic grounds could we judge whether it was great literature. In *The Princess Casamassima* we have the Jamesian ethic applied to the study of the progress of political radicalism in the mind of one young man.

The Jamesian ethic is essentially a Kantian ethic; it deals in self-awareness and the power of "ought." One defines one's own integrity and treats others in terms of that integrity. This is the expression of a Protestant ethic and, as Graham Greene has pointed out, the novel is the Protestant art form.

The Kantian morality is an austere one, and James' characters are cursed with their categorical imperatives. George Eliot is one of James' predecessors in the development of the novel as a study in the consciousness of an ethical dilemma. In a famous statement to F. W. H. Myers, she summed up her own, and James', sense of the ethic with which the novel was to deal, "God is inconceivable, immortality is unbelievable, but duty is peremptory and absolute." Shatov would have understood the statement and it is an antecedent of Hyacinth's declaration: "Does it alter my sacred vow? There are some things in which one can't change. I didn't promise to believe; I promised to obey." The logic of this ethic is that any action is to be weighed against an ideal to determine its value. Hyacinth's problem is that he cannot focus on an ideal; is it his own, or Amanda's, or Christina's, or Paul's or Millicent's, or Mr. Vetch's, or Hoffendahl's? Is he bound by the ideal of culture or of anarchy? He is pledged to one and loves the other. Unwilling to be a traitor, he works out his own solution.

The ethical choice in *The Princess Casamassima* comes with melodramatic trappings, but James is the product of the age of melodrama. The first climax of the novel occurs during a performance of *The Pearl of Paraguay* when the intrigue in the stalls matches that on stage. A mysterious female summons the poor but handsome young man to her box in the theatre. James is doing what he does throughout his career: transforming the conventions of melodrama into high art. The summons, the intrigue, the speculations contrast sharply with the austere morality which informs them. James saw Hyacinth's fate as the dilemma of every sensitive citizen in an age of political melodrama.

The essential James tragedy is that of the man, or woman, who imagines an ideal and lives up to it, only to have that triumph turn to ashes in his mouth. There may somewhere be a place where the good, the true, and the beautiful are integrated and where relationships are authentic; but not in this world and not in this novel.

"Integrated" and "authentic" are curious words. They have an aesthetic connotation, yet they describe qualities we want in political and personal experiences, in rulers and friends. But our problem, like Hamlet's and Hyacinth's, is to determine for ourselves the integrated and authentic when our experience is almost always of the separation of the attractive and the moral. We are fascinated by Christina Light even when we know what she is, and we can never really respond to Lady Aurora despite her good works. Christina is not totally depraved and Lady Aurora is not totally disinterested. Such knowledge is not enough, however, to save Hyacinth.

Running through all of James' work is a special symbol for the inauthentic life: the relationship of one person to another *in loco parentis*. Following his American master, Hawthorne, James saw the terrible sin of the domination of one person over another. Those who dominate in James' world are those who wish to live vicariously, who try to act out some unfulfilled expectation in another. Real parents do this all the time, but James did not write family tragedies. His sinners are those who act *in loco parentis*, who take upon themselves the awful burden of directing another's destiny. With love it may be done, but it is never done without cost. At some point, of course, the person acting in this way will betray or turn upon the other who claims the total support the parent figure offered.

This theme, consistent in James from *Washington Square* to *The Wings of the Dove*, has its roots in his own family experience. That experience looms large in *The Princess Casamassima* in which the recently orphaned Henry created Hyacinth, used his radical sister Alice as a model for the conservative Rosy Muniment, and channeled his complex feelings about his brother William into the creation of Paul Muniment. But the fruits of the feelings are more permanent and more available than the origins.

Hyacinth Robinson has more surrogate fathers and mothers than any other character in fiction. His real father, never absolutely identified, is putatively Lord Frederick Purvis. Hyacinth creates a father from speculation, rumor and even, perhaps, wish. His mother is Florentine Vivier, a French seamstress. She dies in the prison hospital after seeing only once the frightened child she brought into the world.

Acting for one of them at various times in the novel are Mr. Vetch, Paul Muniment, Mr. Crookenden, Eustache Poupin, Hoffendahl, and the unnamed duke designated for assassination. Of mothers, Hyacinth has more than enough: Amanda Pynsent, Mme. Poupin, Florentine Vivier, Millicent Henning, and Christina Light. As he remarks late in the novel, "It's a pity I've always been so terribly under the influence of women. . . ."

In loco parentis is both a private and a public theme in *The Princess Casamassima*. The private or domestic theme involves Hyacinth and women, all of those surrogate mothers.

The private parental theme is sexual. For reasons that will always be obscure, James uses a strange set of images to describe Hyacinth. At one point he is engaged in a brief argument with Rosy Muniment and Paul, in calming him, says, "Why do you want to poke your head into ugly black holes?" Earlier in the novel, Mrs. Bowerbank, the female guard from Florentine's prison, looks at the young Hyacinth and says to Amanda, "You'll find he's big enough, I expect, when he begins to go." At the climax of the novel, when Hyacinth shouts that he is not afraid, that he is as good as any man, and makes his public declaration of total submission to the cause, "he found he had himself sprung up on a chair." This last I take as a metaphor for an erection, for Hyacinth's enlargement of himself, the manning of "little Hyacinth" amid the men in the pub, as he places himself at the disposal of the movement. Politics, not women, seems to get this response from a young man whose name is that of a flower shaped like a phallus.

There are a number of possible interpretations to this pattern of phallic references connected with Hyacinth and more than one is clearly applicable to the novel. I want to concentrate on the connection of the phallic references to the theme of *in loco parentis*. Hyacinth is strangely asexual in the book. He "walks out" with Millicent and lives in the same house with Christina, yet he seems to have no sexual relations. Anger and doubt are two causes of impotence, and Hyacinth, after the terrible encounter with his mother in prison, has more than his share of both.

His tragedy is his divided heritage of fine consciousness and limited prospect. That division manifests itself even in the most intimate parts of being. Because women are, for him, so often surrogate mothers, his only erection comes when he makes a promise to revenge his real mother, and himself, upon his "father." In this way, the private psychology of Hyacinth becomes linked to the world of terror politics. James is not simply identifying sexual impotence with political terrorism; he is leading the reader, more subtly than he did in *The Bostonians,* to consider the ways in which private desires and public attitudes create and re-create each other in the individual mind.

The sexual, the domestic, the private worlds of Hyacinth are dominated by his surrogate mothers. The public worlds of politics, commerce, and art are dominated by his surrogate fathers. Hyacinth takes seriously the radical oratory of these parents. From Mr. Vetch and M. Poupin, he learns to articulate his anger at his dispossessed state. They are the parlor radicals who espouse social action and through them he meets Paul Muniment. He is, in fact, passed from one to the other as he grows older and deeper into the movement. Hyacinth also goes beyond each of them in appreciation of the world and awareness of its impending destruction. The quality of going beyond what has been given him singles out Hyacinth for his mission and his tragedy. He is the son who surpasses the father up to the point at which he is required to kill his father.

Hyacinth's relations with his surrogate parents are part of

his quest for his authentic inheritance and, like Robin's search for his kinsman, they reveal the political world of the novel. From his multinational set of parents, teachers, and guardians Hyacinth learns that he has to define for himself a place in the world. From them, too, he learns that he is "noble" and part of his quest is to authenticate his nobility. The Princess has a title but is not noble. Hoffendahl is the nobility of the movement to which Hyacinth vows his loyalty. Rosy Muniment holds court like a queen and Paul Muniment is clearly an aristocrat of talent. Lady Aurora is noble in spite of her nobility. Medley cries out for a noble tenant. Hyacinth realizes on his grand tour that the "Veronese ceiling" is noble and part of his inheritance. Even Mme. Grandoni and the Prince contribute something to Hyacinth's sense of nobility and inheritance. By the end of the novel, Hyacinth has become so aware of the complex nature of his inheritance that he realizes he must in one way or another be disloyal. Rather than be the "traitor" mentioned in his letter from Venice, he kills himself.

All political literature involves some question of treason, the haunting human problem of loyalty to whom and to what. Dante, countryman of Machiavelli, placed in the pit of Hell three traitors to God and country. The difficult moral questions are of obligation, loyalty, responsibility. Hyacinth did not promise to believe, he promised to obey, and he cannot face the betrayal of his vow or himself.

Graham Greene, one of the best critics of James, writes in *The Lost Childhood* of James' obsession with the "Judas complex":

> Some of James' critics have preferred to ignore the real destiny of characters. . . . he has been multitudinously discussed as a social novelist primarily concerned with the international scene, with the impact of the Old World on the New. . . . No, it was only on the superficial level that James was interested in the American visitor; what deeply interested him, what was indeed his ruling passion, was the idea of treachery, the "Judas complex."

Greene goes on to say that the destiny which James' characters confront is "betrayal." "As he proceeded in his career he shed the more obvious melodramatic trappings of betrayal, and in *The Portrait of a Lady* melodrama is at the point of vanishing. What was to follow was to be only the turning of the screw. Isabel Archer was betrayed by little more than an acquaintance; Milly Theale by her dearest friend; until we reach the complicated culmination of treacheries in *The Golden Bowl*."

Hyacinth in two crucial scenes in *The Princess Casamassima* seems almost like a child spying on his parents as they make love. Perhaps that is the only way James can convey his sense of what Hyacinth feels as a betrayal. Looking at Paul and Christina and then at Sholto and Millicent finishes him. His vow left no room for personal passion and watching the lovers he can only feel betrayed, foolish and totally alone. He has neither parents, nor friends, nor even coconspirators.

In *The Princess Casamassima* James set out to write about terrorism and anarchists and wrote instead about personal loyalty. In a world with no religious sanctions and no moral absolutes, his protagonist must define for himself those values, the state or the self, economics or aesthetics, and those persons, parents, rulers or lovers, to whom he will, if tested, give full allegiance. Faced with his assigned task of assassination, for which he is the most "aesthetically" qualified of the anarchists, Hyacinth must declare his allegiance. He tries to avoid the choice—his seeking out of Millicent—but cannot and then he commits suicide. James' special contribution to our political education was the re-creation of the agony of consciousness in a sensitive man faced with the inevitability of treason.

The novel opens and closes with a woman looking for Hyacinth; in between he finds himself. In the process he answers the question first put to him by Lady Aurora in the Muniment flat, ". . . how far exactly do you go?" Later in the novel Hyacinth says to the Princess, "You do go too far." She replies, "looking at him musingly: 'How *can* one, after all, go too far? That's the word of cowards.'" The question haunts James and his novel. The world is corrupt and needs reform but what then is justifiable for any one person?

In a remarkable passage early in the novel Amanda Pynsent, in her innocence, touches the political heart of the novel. As she looks at the prison to which she has brought Hyacinth so that his wretched mother may see him, James says:

> It looked very sinister and wicked, to Miss Pynsent's eyes, and she wondered why a prison should have such an evil air if it was erected in the interest of justice and order—a builded protest, precisely, against vice and villainy. This particular penitentiary struck her as about as bad and wrong as those who were in it; it threw a blight on the face of day, making the river seem foul and poisonous and the opposite bank, with a protrusion of long-necked chimneys, unsightly gasometers and deposits of rubbish. wear the aspect of a region at whose expense the jail had been populated.

Amanda's very Dickensian thoughts are the source of the questions which run throughout the book, the questions of political consciousness. Given the prison and Medley, two great dwellings which Hyacinth visits in the novel, what are the possibilities for the society in which both exist? Based on his knowledge of both, what is Hyacinth justified in doing? The beginning of morality in political relationships is the question: how far exactly do you go?

At the end of the novel Hyacinth has nowhere to go. Politics and people have failed him and there is only his sense of duty to sustain him. Mme. Grandoni had warned him: "Don't give up *yourself*," but when he sees Millicent with Sholto he has no choice. Because he believes that thoughts have consequences, he is the ideal subject for a novel. Because he feels that political beliefs require action, he is the ideal center of consciousness for the novel James wanted. Too involved personally for the rhetorical revolution of Poupin, he certainly cannot, like the Princess, dabble in radicalism. His seriousness is his strength and his vulnerability. This seriousness enables him to see in Medley a "serenity of success, an accumulation of dignity and honour." Christina, the frantic dilettante, can appreciate its convenience, "before we blow it up." It was the guilty dabblers of Christina's class and not the serious anarchists who, some twenty-five years after the novel, did blow up all that dignity and honor.

I said sometime before that James was too great a novelist and too great a moralist to deal in stark polarities. In *The Princess Casamassima*, the noble and the base in the aristocracy and the proletariat are presented in a mixture that allows no easy judgments. To make the tragedy complete, however, James gives Hyacinth an alternative to the class conflict in his world and in his soul. At the beginning of the fifth book, Hyacinth has a place in the world and "prospects." His seriousness and his concern for craft make him the most promising employee in Mr. Crookenden's establishment. He is offered a place in the bourgeois world and, possibly, the hand of the boss's daughter. Hyacinth cannot accept this compromise but its possibility helps define the starkness of his choice. Conrad, later, would make his special subject the politics of success and the morality of achievement.

Christina Light has the best line in the book: "You know people oughtn't to be both corrupt and dreary." The noble radical who has married her title is addressing the aristocratic nihilist who cannot inherit his. The line involves the mixture of moral and aesthetic standards on which the novel is based. It is a fine Jamesian irony that gives the line to Christina. The artist knew that if political action is limited to an affirmation of either the corrupt or the dreary, then civilization is doomed.

That contrast is implicit in the quotation with which this

chapter opens. For some reason, the post-industrial West has assumed an opposition between the moral (full employment) and the aesthetic (*Oedipus* and *Hamlet*). James knew that the social order in which they are opposed can only destroy the individuals trying to exist in it. His effort in the novel is to encompass in an act of the imagination the tragedy of the working class and the tragedy of Hamlet. If he had no real knowledge of the radical underworld, he had the daily newspapers and what he called in his Preface "the penetrating imagination." He knew, better than John Morley or his sister Alice, the degree to which an aesthetic concept—imagination—shaped both the tragedy of Hamlet and the tragedy of the working man.

James is the moralist he is because he is able to represent in his fiction the destructive power of a virtue. The very imagination praised in the Preface is part of the problem of the characters. The novelist imagines Hyacinth's world because he does not know it first hand. He writes his own problem into his book by having the characters live in terms of some kind of imagination; they "suppose" and "imagine" throughout the book. Rosy, Millicent, and Amanda live in terms of an aristocratic world they create in their fantasy. Christina creates a proletariat which will thrill her more than the stuffy aristocracy she knows. To complete a fantasy, they create worlds that are more important to them than any reality. Hyacinth, the little bookbinder on whom nothing is lost, can, like Hamlet, imagine consequences and his imagination is what distinguishes and destroys him.

Graham Greene pointed out that betrayal was the subject that obsessed the artist, and Pound said that freedom and bondage were James' great themes. The very words—freedom, bondage, betrayal—are political words and in a group of novels in the eighties, *The Bostonians, The Princess Casamassima* and *The Tragic Muse,* James was overtly political in his subject matter. Read with the great critical faculty of hindsight, *The Princess Casamassima* deals clearly with the issues that led finally to the disaster of 1914. But these issues are dealt with in terms of James' special kind of history—the history of fine consciousness.

Hyacinth knew some possibility of liberty until, "he gave Hoffendahl a mortgage on it." The novel deals with many kinds of bondage: the bondage of poverty and class, of love and responsibility, of a political ideal. Because he deals so well with consciousness, it has too often been assumed that James was unaware of history. What we learn again in *The Princess Casamassima* is how political events are the sum of individual decisions and that political action, as distinct from political talk, requires some expenditure of the self. What we dread as moral beings is that acting to affirm some belief will cost us not less than everything else we cherish.

Chapter Five

Conrad: The Price of Politics

HEART OF DARKNESS is like another story well-told, *The Rime of the Ancient Mariner*. A sailor has taken a strange voyage, seen and done strange things, been changed, and now, to an unwilling audience, he will report what he has learned.

Heart of Darkness is also like another nineteenth-century story of a quest by water, *Moby Dick*. Taken together these novels are the tragic epics of trade.

At the core of both *Heart of Darkness* and *Moby Dick* is the story of a private adventure within a commercial venture in which success at trade is the excuse for the realization of a dream. Kurtz is like Ahab, the Marlow like Ishmael. Kurtz and Ahab are consumed by their vision; Ishmael and Marlow survive, both saved by luck and by the vagueness of their purpose.

The narrators are not driven men, but restless men who want to go to sea. They are witnesses who are not destroyed in the realization of some "higher" purpose and who survive the tragic events because their very lack of purpose exempts them from the tragic rhythm. The "idea" which alone, Marlow says, redeems the commercial enterprise, also, as both Ishmael and Marlow learn, damns. Both bring back from their voyages the priceless treasure of painful knowledge.

In *Moby Dick* and *Heart of Darkness*, the narrators show

us the dark and mysterious places of the human heart. They do it by showing the motives beneath the deeds, motives that are not only those of individuals, but of an entire civilization. Both novels deal with the drive of pride and power, of greed and conviction of righteousness, called "manifest destiny." In nineteenth-century studies that dramatic phrase need not be limited to American history. "Manifest destiny" is an appropriate phrase for the force of belief that drove Americans, Englishmen, Russians, Germans, and Frenchmen beyond their borders in the name of the great Jehovah, steam power, and the sanctity of trade. To understand *Moby Dick* and *Heart of Darkness,* and after them *Nostromo,* is to understand that manifest destiny is the public statement of an idea which damned or redeemed with remarkable unconcern for the human actors in the drama.

Using Ezra Pound's definition of poetry—*language charged with meaning to the utmost possible degree*—*Heart of Darkness* is a very poetic novel. White men go into the blackness of the jungle represented by a white space on the map to subjugate black men in order to extract the white treasure, ivory. Only in a novel so completely realized would the company doctor in Brussels and Kurtz at the Inner Station, both employees of the grand, civilizing, trading venture, be so interested in heads. Marlow, like Ishmael and the Mariner, tells his story because he has learned something about himself and about every man. His story is that of a man's journey into the self and the discovery of the darkness that is there. The image is close to that of Dostoyevsky, whom Conrad did not like, in *Notes From Underground,* the story from the mousehole, jottings from the space beneath the floorboards. These explorations of the darkness within are central documents in modernism. But *Heart of Darkness* has an explicitly public theme: the exploration of the darkness at the heart of civilization. I want to concentrate on the political rather than the psychological theme, and on the substance of the tale, the mythology which the poetry re-creates.

That public theme is, of course, imperialism. Conrad had

already said, in the note prefaced to *The Nigger of the Narcissus*, that the responsibility of the artist is to make us "see." He meant the rich doubleness of the English "to see," present to the senses and comprehended by the intellect. Conrad's intention and his achievement in *Heart of Darkness* is to make us "see"—i.e., to understand more fully—the historical abstraction called imperialism in its very human forms. He even provides a dramatic model. Marlow, in the grove of death, acts out the reader's response, seeing more and more clearly in the darkness of the trees until he finally discerns the human face of the commercial adventure. That act stands for the story itself in which Conrad makes us see the men who created and left to us the abstractions of history. Recent events indicate that we study well neither our history nor our art.

Conrad's imperial theme has three dimensions—historical, economic and national—all contained in a unifying myth. The historical comes first, with the evocation early in the novel of Rome and its far-flung empire. Rome, once a great imperial power, has vanished; and London, now the center of commerce and civilization, was once an obscure outpost of progress on the dark edge of the world. The sense that empires flourish and fail, and that the end of the nineteenth century might be the beginning of the end of one more period of enlightened expansion is implicit in Marlow's dramatic opening, "And this also . . . has been one of the dark places of the earth."

Marlow's listeners represent the second dimension of the imperial theme, the economic. Gathered on the yawl with Marlow and the other narrator are a banker, an accountant, and a director of companies. Like Bildad and Peleg in *Moby Dick*, they ship only in home waters, these patricians safe in the capital while others live and work in loneliness at the Inner Stations of the world. These captains of commerce are the counterparts of the traders, managers, and accountants Marlow has met in the Congo. It is for the comfort and profit of those aboard the *Nellie* that others sail in less well-appointed ships up the Congo and across the seas. These careful men of business do not really want to know of the waste, the murder, the insane greed at the other end of the world, at the other end of the process which makes their lives possible.

The third element in Conrad's imperial theme is the national. *Heart of Darkness* begins on the Thames, just off London, with the English and soon includes Belgians, a French gunboat, a Swedish captain, a Russian harlequin and, of course, the Africans. Perhaps the most pregnant line in this pregnant story is that which says quietly, "All Europe contributed to the making of Kurtz." With the same kind of uncanny prophecy Dostoyevsky put into *The Possessed,* Conrad looks to the future, to the darkness about to erupt from the heart of Europe, and the darkness in the hearts of men. Imperialism is a product of triumphant nationalism. Triumphant nationalism begets conquest, which begets nationalist rebellion, in what the exiled Pole saw as an endless cycle.

The imperial theme, in all its aspects, is what Conrad wants us to see. Marlow deals not with yarns, but with myths; not with stories, but with those ideas that lead men into the heart of darkness.

The central myth of *Heart of Darkness* is one that has shaped much of modern history. It may be expressed in a simple equation:

$$C_1 + C_2 = C_3$$

The notation means Christianity plus Commerce equals Civilization. The equation stands for the belief which, since 1492, has largely determined the shape of the world. Conrad, like Euripides at the end of another mythic and imperialistic age, makes a religious belief the subject of his novel. $C_1 + C_2 = C_3$ is the formula for the myth, the myth is the subject of the story, and Marlow and Kurtz are the human actors who represent to us the tragedy of history.

Kurtz, Marlow, and the other inhabitants of the stations stand for the thousands of other men—those Caucasians, averaging five feet eight inches in height, from the small European peninsula attached to the Asian land mass and from some islands off its coast, who, between 1500 and 1900, conquered the world. The high point of this incredible expansion was the nineteenth century for which the American experience, the conquest of a continent and the subjugation of a race, is an appropriate symbol. Conrad's subject is the human meaning of this expansionism, its sources and effects in the minds of the men who lived it.

From the discovery of America to the outbreak of World War I, European expansion is motivated by the "idea" to which Marlow refers, the idea which combines God and Mammon and leads men to tame a wilderness. One must, the simplified belief has it, conquer the unconquered land in order to establish trade and convert the heathens. Converting the heathens is a noble, spiritual enterprise. Trade will prosper as a sign of God's blessing on the enterprise. To the adherents of the myth, the white man's burden was the white man's glory. The expansion of the European nations in Africa in the nineteenth century was the working out of the Protestant Ethic in global terms, and in that sense Tawney's *Religion and the Rise of Capitalism* and Weber's *The Protestant Ethic and the Spirit of Capitalism* are better guides to Conrad's story than many works of literary criticism.

Heart of Darkness is a bitter parody of the success story. The pattern Conrad is manipulating is that of the biography of the young man who is talented but not immediately successful at home; he goes to a strange land, overcomes great obstacles, and returns rich and famous to win the girl. In Conrad's version, however, there are two protagonists and the plot is more complicated: Kurtz acts out the purpose and the passion of the tragedy; Marlow shadows these and then returns to the Intended with a new perception of himself and the world. He is our necessary witness to the tragedy.

Kurtz and Marlow discover that imperialism never really worked anyway. But myths work on promise, not performance, and believers try to separate their motives from their deeds: "Of course you must take care of the motives—right motives—always," is what the raving Kurtz says to Marlow. At the end of the great century of expansion, Conrad makes clear the reality which the myth was meant to cover: money and guns, not contracts and crosses, made the Caucasians prevail. Kurtz is the Belgians in the Congo, the French in Algeria, the Americans in Vietnam. His collapse is the collapse of colonialism.

His end, however, is neither simple nor abstract. Kurtz is, even in his corruption—"my ivory"—so much more fascinating than the lukewarm time-servers that we must, with Marlow, identify with him. Kurtz is a man who set out to validate the myth in his own person and did not accept the pious statements as an excuse for greed. At the Inner Station, from being too much "alone" and too much adored, he came to see the meaning of the myth as "the horror." Yet his fall moves us, and in his despair there remains something of the noble purpose—the bringing of light to the darkness. It is to that that Marlow is faithful because, apparently, the alternative is pillage with no hope of redemption.

F. R. Leavis, otherwise an excellent critic of Conrad, complains of a fuzziness at the center of the story and objects to Conrad's adjectival insistence on profundity. As applied to *Heart of Darkness,* fuzzy is a descriptive but only partially an evaluative term. Conrad is dealing with myths, dreams, and "ideas" and, as Kurtz learns, these should perhaps be left fuzzy If they are, then the Belgian owners and the bookkeeper, the director of companies, the lawyer, and the accountant can continue to work. In *Moby Dick,* Bildad and Peleg, the pious owners of the Pequod, send men on a voyage to hell while they remain carefully uninformed about the sordid details of their noble enterprise. To try to live the dream is destructive and bad for business: Kurtz spoils the territory and Ahab loses a cargo of oil and the ship. The moral fable of *Heart of Darkness* is not fuzzy; man's aspirations are ambiguous. Kurtz does accomplish his purpose; he sets up a beacon in the darkness by the light of which we can see clearly "the horror, the horror."

Conrad writes so well of this tragic dilemma because he felt it so personally. Like Marlow, he had to be loyal to the nightmare of his choice. He could, for example, regard the merchant service as a creation of man in which moral order was possible, but he knew that the merchant service served the capitalist Mammon like a Seraphic host.

Heart of Darkness came to be written because on his own journey up the great, snake-like river, Conrad saw the tragic consequences of noble intentions. His task as an artist was to make us see. No one, especially no American, can encounter for the first or fiftieth time that solitary French gunboat lying off the impenetrable jungle shelling the "enemy" without some shiver of recognition. As Wyndham Lewis said, artists write the history of the future.

———◆———

The subject of *Nostromo* is the creation of the Occidental Republic, an enlightened, solvent, progressive modern nation. That tragedy comprises a number of individual tragedies.

In *Heart of Darkness* the emphasis is on a private self trying to understand its world and on private experience in contrast with public belief, slogans, and stated aspirations. The emphasis in *Nostromo* is on the public world. Although few novels take us further inside more characters, the focus is on the web of public actions and political beliefs which shape and change the motives of the characters. Private feelings of love and hate, all intimate human desires, are sucked into the political realities of Sulaco and are altered. The world of the novel and the state created in *Nostromo* are the modern political country in which we experience ourselves as aliens.

In his letters and conversations, Conrad's references to Dostoyevsky are barely civil. Struggling toward his ideal of a novel as a complexly wrought thing, he would have little aesthetic patience for the Russian. More important, Conrad, a Pole, could have little good to say for the spokesman for Russia triumphant, when the fruits of that triumph included the crushing of Polish independence and the destruction of Conrad's immediate family. Differing so profoundly from each other, the novelists did share a sense of the political questions with which fiction could deal. *The Possessed* and *The Legend of the Grand Inquisitor, Heart of Darkness* and *Nostromo* all focus on the crucial question of modern politics: what frees?

In *Nostromo* this question is posed in terms that are very human. In what can one believe, in order to have the sense of freedom men say they want and which our political order is meant to insure? Is there any freedom in the poverty and disease of the underdeveloped country; is there more in a smoothly functioning corporate state? Is there freedom in allegiance to a church, spiritual values, or an ennobling idea? In human feeling or in a social program? In activism or in thought? In money or in love?

This is the painful litany of partial answers to the question "what frees" by the citizens and sojourners in the province of Sulaco that becomes the Occidental Republic. Each character tries to find freedom in the terms just proposed. However unsatisfactory, the terms are difficult to do without. The national story is the analogue for all personal stories: the struggle to become free, independent, and secure. What we watch in the novel is each character becoming trapped in his efforts to free himself, his country or both.

Perhaps, however, "What frees?" is the wrong question. Conrad, standing apart from his characters and not sharing Dostoyevsky's belief in a national sanctity that frees, seems to ask, in his creative pessimism, what sustains? The answer, that of Captain Mitchell, is unimaginative self-assurance to the point of unconsciousness. It works for him. Most of Conrad's characters are more like Prince Hamlet than Captain Mitchell and are sustained only by questioning anything that sustains. To the question what can sustain a conscious man, Conrad's answer seems to be agnostic faith or skeptical illusion. But few, if any, people can sustain themselves in this way, and we watch them in the novel, the imaginative characters, as they harden or crumble while trying to maintain by themselves the will to believe. For Conrad the sustaining force seems to be some combination of Hyacinth Robinson's, "I promised to obey, I didn't promise to believe," and Shatov's, "I will believe . . . I will believe in God." Conrad's answer is irony at the moment of affirmation—for those for whom this is possible. *Nostromo* shows the noble and the base actions of men and women in the creation of a modern state. In that state nothing frees and nothing sustains, except, for the lucky ones, a willed illusion.

The myth which informs *Heart of Darkness*, the myth of imperialism and its equation of Christianity, Commerce and Civilization, is also the myth of *Nostromo*. The nineteenth is the special century of that equation, and the novels are products of Conrad's experience in that period of inspired expansion. The myth was operating from at least the fifteenth century in shaping the course of history, but the difference in the nineteenth century was power—the direct application of enormous power to political, social, and economic problems. The invention of new forms of power and applications of power in its crudest and subtlest forms is the history of the century and Lord Acton had only to look around for the inspiration for his famous epigram.

In the nineteenth century, political power became clearly

and completely an extension of technological power. The steamboat and the Gatling gun, the telegraph, the railroad, and the revolver helped make imperialism possible and then necessary. Technology was the vehicle of expansionist political dreams and for the development of the nation-state as a repository of power for aggressive self-defense. The armaments industry and the armaments race which made World War I inevitable were the products of a technology made to serve political orders which had no values other than the exercise of power. In the absence of restraining values, the only value is the logic of technology itself, the logic of Frankenstein. Modern politics is the politics of power. Perhaps there never was any other kind, but by the end of the nineteenth century the triumph of technology represented the triumph of the mentality of power.

The technologist works to harness, to subdue, to create processes which will predict and control. Some men recognized that, if one could control natural processes, one could also control men. One aim of technological power is, obviously, the transcending of human limitations. The discovery that a stone axe is less vulnerable than a hand is one of the first such acts of transcendence. But after the Renaissance and its demon figure of Faustus in search of knowledge as power, the transcendence of individual limits through the application of power became the theme of politics. The nation can then be defined as the embodiment of an individual will to power: Napoleon. Or, technological power becomes an instrument for imposing an individual will upon a nation: Hitler, for example, is not possible without a microphone.

The paradox in all of this is represented by the contrast of Marlowe's and Goethe's Faust. Man's effort has always been to transcend himself and Goethe's Faust discovers that salvation is striving. Somewhere along the way, however, the notion of striving and salvation, of success and going beyond, became confused. Going beyond limits became identified with amassing—a personal fortune or a colonial empire—and the spiritual sense of transcendence became confused with the capitalist sense of aggrandizement. The nation-state began to act like a capitalist and transcended its boundaries in order to make more secure the power base which helped create the boundaries. The nation-state became a Marlovian character—an "overreacher," and that is the meaning of imperialism.

For the true believer, the whole process was part of a divine plan: Holroyd, the American financier of the San Tomé mine, can calmly say, "We shall run the world's business whether the world likes it or not. The world can't help it—and neither can we, I guess." For this Napoleon of industry, the advance of enlightened capitalism is inevitable. His secret, and Charles Gould's, is the belief that this progress really has divine sanction. Conrad presents Holroyd as follows: "his massive profile was the profile of a Caesar's head on an old Roman coin." This is one of the countless Biblical references in Conrad's anti-Gospel; the original is Christ's statement about the coin of tribute: "Render, therefore, to Caesar the things that are Caesar's, and to God, the things that are God's." For the new Puritans, Holroyd and Gould, the text is sanction, and they can claim the earth and everything in it in the name of Caesar and God. As Conrad says of Holroyd, his heritage gave him "the temperament of a Puritan and an insatiable imagination of conquest."

Conrad deals in myth because only myth can encompass the story he wants to tell. He sets out to narrate the events surrounding the creation of a small but rich republic in South America, through the intervention of Anglo-Saxon technology and money which intervention is motivated by a Puritan desire for worldly success as a symbol for redemption. Conrad's artistic conscience required that he submit myths to a withering investigation. His irony in *Nostromo* is turned upon the creation myth: the making of the modern world in the wreckage of a decayed feudalism. That is why Nostromo, awakening after his long sleep, appears as a new Adam: he is about to enter a completely new world. He enters it already guilty of sin.

In Nostromo's world, political power comes from technological power, from the ability to control processes. One of the most arresting elements in *Nostromo* is its treatment of the theme of technological power, symbolized by the lighthouse, the dynamite at the mine, Captain Mitchell's gold chronometer, and the telephone by which Charles Gould informs Emilia that he will not sleep beside her because he must stay and attend to some trouble at the mine.

In *Heart of Darkness*, the technology does not work: the broken pipes, the sunken boat, the missing rivets, the troublesome boiler are its symbols. Only the whistle and the guns seem really effective. In the earlier story, Conrad is fascinated with imperialism as a destructive force and represents it with the gunboat senselessly shelling the jungle and the ugly stations of death strewn on the face of the land. Imperialism is not the noble mission it is made to seem in Brussels, the city of whited sepulchres; it is rape and desecration. Kurtz is right in believing that the vast commercial undertaking can only be redeemed by the "idea." As Marlow says:

> The conquest of the earth, which mostly means the taking it away from those who have a different complexion or slightly flatter noses than ourselves, is not a pretty thing when you look into it too much. What redeems it is the idea only.

Nostromo, as Robert Penn Warren noted, is also concerned with the redeeming idea. But *Nostromo* is a different work, set in a different world, and the technology works only too well. In *Nostromo*, Conrad turns his corrosive irony on the redeeming idea itself. Not the idea corrupted, not the idea failed, not the idea betrayed, but the idea fulfilled is his subject—and that is the source of the terrible bitterness, of the total irony of the book.

In *Nostromo*, Conrad is still aware of the destructive force of technological power but he treats it in a different way.

The waterfall existed no longer. The tree-ferns that had luxuriated in its spray had dried around the dried up pool, and the high ravine was only a big trench half filled up with the refuse of excavations and tailings. The torrent, damned up above, sent its water rushing along the open flumes of scooped tree-trunks striding on trestle legs to the turbines working the stamps on the lower plateau—the *mesa grande* of the San Tomé mountain. Only the memory of the waterfall, with its amazing fernery, like a hanging garden above the rocks of the gorge, was preserved in Mrs. Gould's water-color sketch; she had made it hastily one day from a cleared patch in the bushes, sitting in the shade of a roof of straw erected for her on three rough poles under Don Pépé's direction.

The waterfall has been replaced by ore shoots, and the changed sound has special meaning for the man who made it: "To Charles Gould's fancy it seemed that the sound must reach the uttermost limits of the province . . . , it came to his heart with the peculiar force of a proclamation thundered forth over the land and the marvelousness of an accomplished fact fulfilling an audacious desire." Charles Gould does not mean, as do the station managers, to rape the earth for profit. He means to create a good state in the Costaguana where he was born. For him the myth still works; it is still $C_1 + C_2 = C_3$. Technology is the instrument of commerce, and commerce is the lifeblood of civilization. Commerce means order, and order is morality. Only reluctantly does he come to realize that technology can serve war as well as trade. The point of the waterfall passage quoted above is not that Conrad is an ecologist ahead of his time, but that he saw the meaning of the rape of the earth and knew that if the redeeming idea was based on it, the idea would not work. Charles Gould thinks of himself as the savior of his country, but mining the minerals of the earth puts him irretrievably in the devil's party.

Technology is part of the political question which involves all of the characters in the novel: who shall have power in Sulaco? General Barrios, armed with the new rifles Decoud brought from Europe, returns to defeat Pedrito Montero, summoned by Nostromo who made his way free on a railroad engine. Barrios saves the province for the mine, and it is the lights of the mine that dominate the Occidental Republic. The role of the mine and its technology in creating and sustaining that republic is clear: money is converted to machinery, which converts the earth to money as profit, which is converted to political power by some form of bribery, either extortion or influence.

The Sam Tomé mine is the obvious symbol of the relation of technology and ideology in the novel, but Conrad uses instruments on a more human scale. He does this for the same reason that he tells his story of the complete history of a country in intimate scenes involving only two characters; he is concerned to show the human effects of service to any ideology.

Late in the novel, after the revolution and American intervention have created the Occidental Republic, after the arrival of the tram cars in what Captain Mitchell describes as an enlightened spot in a turbulent continent, Charles and Emilia Gould return from a vacation in Europe. Charles rushes off to the mine. Emilia and Doctor Monygham are together; she devoted to her absent husband and the doctor to her. A servant enters:

> "What is it, Basilio?" asked Mrs. Gould.
> "A telephone came through from the office of the mine. The master remains to sleep at the mountain to-night."

The only words spoken after this dismiss the servant—" 'Very well, Basilio,' said Mrs. Gould"—and the next three pages are given to Mrs. Gould's thoughts, until, at last, she stammers, "Material interests."

The telephone, as much as the message it carries, is the symbol of the failure in the success of the idea. In Charles Gould's triumphant reckoning the telephone should represent

peace, progress, prosperity, order, and fulfillment. Yet it
serves here to separate the Goulds and validate the prophecy
Monygham has just made:

> "Will there be never any peace? Will there be no rest?" Mrs.
> Gould whispered. "I thought that we—"
> "No!" interrupted the doctor. "There is no peace and rest
> in the development of material interests. They have their law
> and their justice. But it is founded on expediency, and is
> inhuman; it is without rectitude, without the continuity and
> the force that can be found only in a moral principle. Mrs.
> Gould, the time approaches when all that the Gould Con-
> cession stands for shall weigh as heavily upon the people as
> the barbarism, cruelty, and misrule of a few years back."

The sad history of imperialism is witness to the accuracy
of the doctor's chilling statement. After the telephone call,
just some trouble with the workers at the mine, Emilia Gould
knows that the doctor is right; "She saw the San Tomé mountain hanging over the Campo, over the whole land, feared,
hated, wealthy, more soulless than any tyrant, more pitiless
and autocratic than the worst government, ready to crush
innumerable lives in the expansion of its greatness." But she
goes on to think of her husband, "He did not see it. He could
not see it. It was not his fault. He was perfect." She will not
see the madness of a man who deserts his wife and seeks satisfaction in a hole in a mountain. He will, no matter what, sur-
pass his father.

What Monygham cannot see and Emilia will not see is that
for the few, for Charles Gould, Holroyd, and Kurtz, the tragedy is that they thought that their material interests had a
moral force. They never really learn that the forces with
which they deal have a logic beyond man's moral vision.

The doctor's bitter but accurate statement comes at the end
of the story of Charles and Emilia Gould. Earlier in the novel
there is another striking confrontation of the opposing values,
hot and cold, which shape the book. The scene occurs in the
midst of the revolution when the outcome is still in doubt.

At stake is whether Sulaco will be ruled by light orderliness or dark banditry; in the abandoned Customs House the rebel colonel, Sotillo, confronts the imperturbable Anglo-Saxon, Captain Mitchell.

The confrontation begins when Captain Mitchell, seized by Sotillo's troops following their landing in Sulaco after the collision with the lighter of silver, demands the return of his watch which the soldiers have taken. This "sixty-guinea gold half-chronometer presented to him years ago by a committee of underwriters for saving a ship from total loss by fire" is a symbol of the ordered world of commercial integrity that Captain Mitchell inhabits. That world is trying to render its kind of justice to the province it has appropriated but it is threatened by the unruly inhabitants to whom the good is being done. Sotillo, claiming to be a revolutionary soldier and not a bandit chieftain, has the watch brought to him, holds it, and then becomes fascinated by it. "He became so interested that for an instant he forgot his precious prisoner. There is always something childish in the rapacity of the passionate, clear-minded southern races, wanting in the misty idealism of the notherners, who at the smallest encouragement dream of nothing less than the conquest of the earth."

Sotillo turns again to his prisoner. He must learn where the silver has gone and notices that Captain Mitchell flinches when he accuses him of having spirited it away in a boat.

> "Ha! you tremble!" Sotillo shouted suddenly. "It is a conspiracy. It is a crime against the state. Did you not know that the silver belongs to the republic till the government claims are satisfied? Where is it? Where have you hidden it, you miserable thief?"

Each has now accused the other of being a thief and the distinction is an interesting one. We can recognize the justice in Sotillo's ravings and have to hand the appropriate epithets of exploitation, racism, and imperialism, as well as the charge that the capitalist ethic condones the theft of a country but not of a watch. But the passage defies simplification and is a classic example of what happens when politics is the subject of a novel. Our response to the characters in the scene is more aesthetic than political. Sotillo has a real claim, but he is an unprincipled adventurer. He wants for his own purposes the treasure of Charles Gould, the principled adventurer. More to the point, Sotillo is a sordid, ugly, and repulsive man. Captain Mitchell is not terribly bright and is an agent of the capitalist-imperialist exploiters. Yet, despite his stolid, unimaginative support of the status quo, we like him as a man and, moreover, we too have been caught up in the grand adventure of saving the silver. Thus in this brief scene we are involved in a complex process of political judgment and aesthetic response. We have, in effect, the political novel in miniature.

Captain Mitchell triumphs. He deceives Sotillo, regains his watch, and lives to bore tourists with his account of the historical revolution and then to retire to England. He would be surprised to know of Emilia Gould's bitter conclusion that the triumph was hollow and that others would press Sotillo's claim.

Technological power controls the fate of Sulaco from the very beginning of the book. The opening paragraph of the first chapter of *Nostromo: A Tale of the Seaboard* is:

> In the time of Spanish rule, and for many years afterwards, the town of Sulaco—the luxuriant beauty of the orange gardens bears witness to its antiquity—had never been commercially anything more important than a coasting port with a fairly large local trade in ox-hides and indigo. The clumsy, deep-sea galleons of the conquerors, that, needing a brisk gale to move at all, would lie becalmed, where your modern ship, built on clipper lines, forges ahead by the mere flapping of her sails, had been barred out of Sulaco by the prevailing calms of its vast gulf. Some harbors of the earth are made difficult of access by the treachery of sunken rocks and the tempests of their shores. Sulaco had found an inviolable sanctuary from the temptations of a trading world in the solemn hush of the deep Golfo Placido as if within an enormous semicircular and unroofed temple open to the ocean,

with its walls of lofty mountains hung with the mourning draperies of cloud.

The first chapter introduces us to the geography of Sulaco, some of its history and the great legend of the gringos condemned to live on Azuera in search of an elusive treasure. Conard gives us, in effect, geography, history, and myth—all that is necessary for the making of a state. But some catalyst was missing and that is introduced in the opening paragraph of the second chapter:

> The only sign of commercial activity within the harbor, visible from the beach of the Great Isabel, is the square blunt end of the wooden jetty which the Oceanic Steam Navigation Company (the O.S.N. of familiar speech) had thrown over the shallow part of the bay soon after they had resolved to make of Sulaco one of their ports of call for the republic of Costaguana. The state possesses several harbors on its long seaboard, but except Cayta, an important place, all are either small and inconvenient inlets in an iron-bound coast—like Esmeralda, for instance, sixty miles to the south—or else mere open roadsteads exposed to the winds and fretted by the surf.
>
> Perhaps the very atmospheric conditions which had kept away the merchant fleets of by-gone ages induced the O.S.N. Company to violate the sanctuary of peace sheltering the calm existence of Sulaco. The variable airs sporting lightly with the vast semicircle of waters within the head of Azuera could not baffle the steam power of their excellent fleet.

The words "commercially' and "commercial" are prominent in both openings. Conrad is establishing one element in the equation $C_1 + C_2 = C_3$. Christianity is there. It will get new vigor from Father Corbelàn who, like Kurtz, will go among the natives to convert them, but unlike Kurtz will return to civilization to become a prince of the Church and an ardent defender of its material interests in Sulaco.

Both the medieval and the modern church are represented in the book. Medieval Christianity—the church as opponent of capitalist expansion—is represented by Father Beron, the sadist who breaks Doctor Monygham in an inquisition. A more modern priest is Father Roman, the only man Don Pépé can entrust with the sacred mission of destroying, if necessary, the entire San Tomé mine. Pure Christianity comes with the triumph of capitalism and the missionaries sent from Holroyd. But this Christian history of Sulaco anticipates the commercial history contained in the opening paragraphs quoted.

History is change and the crucial change from the opening of Chapter One to that of Chapter Two is the introduction of steam power. Conrad hated steam powered ships and turned this feeling into a powerful symbol. The whole novel is prefigured in the shift represented by the steam power: the transformation of Sulaco from a quiet port for ox-hides and indigo to a port for the foreign-based, capitalist, dependable, amoral and apolitical "Oceanic Steam Navigation Company (the O.S.N. of familiar speech)." The fable of the gringos destroyed by their search for a treasure is one kind of metonymy for the novel, the steam power of the O.S.N. is another. Ships powered by steam bring foreign capital to Sulaco and the foreigners to make it work; they bring revolutionaries and counterrevolutionaries to Sulaco; they take out silver and bring in guns; an American warship arrives to insure the triumph of Charles Gould as the King of Sulaco, just as the U.S.S. *Nashville* arrived off the coast of Panama to protect the revolution for independence from Colombia and to redeem the fortunes of Ferdinand de Lesseps' old Universal Oceanic Canal Company. In the violence with which the book opens, it is the O.S.N., the dependable line that never loses a package or a man, that saves the fleeing dictator.

Conrad uses, in his special way, a remarkable human symbol for the fate of the country that is determined by the introduction of steam power in Chapter Two. A change is that from trade in ox-hides and indigo to international commerce. Mr. Hirsch is a victim of the change. He is a dealer in hides, the staple of trade before the arrival of the O.S.N.

He is destroyed in his efforts to flee the revolution, killed by the same load of silver that damns Nostromo and Martin Decoud. The pitiful, tortured Hirsch, who is twice the unwilling companion of Nostromo, provokes Sotillo into shooting him in order to end his pain. He is one of the casual casualties in the modernizing of Sulaco, a man lost by the O.S.N. when it lost its only valuable cargo.

But Hirsch is also a Jew. He is an itinerant Jewish trader, probably a peddler remembered from Conrad's Polish boyhood. He is the individual entrepreneur swallowed up in the capitalist expansion. (Charles Gould has no time for him as he thinks of the sanctity of trade and contracts.) He is commerce, not Commerce. He is of the old way, before steam and mass production. He is a figure of the Old Testament and is destroyed in the progress of Gould and Holroyd, the apostles of a pure Christianity.

The dilemma of modern man in the face of his political creations is the gap between public requirements and private feelings; between what is institutionalized and what is yearned for. Our sense is that the political order will never evolve quickly enough to reflect our finest moral perceptions. Irving Howe says of *Nostromo*, "problems of morality and problems of politics . . . seem very much the same." That is because they are the same. A political order defines the public relationships of one person to another; for example, the right to own property in the face of needs of others whether those others are defined singly or as the commonwealth. The public, political world is concerned primarily with action; the novel and psychology with private, often unexpressed, motives. Conrad is concerned with the relation of the two. Thus, in his novel, Charles Gould and Pedrito Montero, politically so opposed, are morally so close. Both wish to preserve the mine, the wealth of Sulaco, and are prepared to let the rest of Costaguana go to hell. Both are brave men, willing to defy odds; the revolutionary and the capitalist are, at heart, adventurers vying for the title of "King of Sulaco."

Moral in politics usually means free from self-interest and

the irony of *Nostromo* is so total because Conrad exposes the private motives for the public deeds. In the process he exposes the problem of politics: how to reconcile the conflicting impulses to selfishness and sacrifice. This private emphasis is the reason *Nostromo,* a national novel of imperialism, is told in such personal terms. Virtually the whole book, for all of its violent background, dramatic and even melodramatic action, consists of scenes of two people in intense private conversation. In these scenes, each character is trying to impress something upon the other, to control the other, to direct the other in some course of action, to persuade, trick, deceive, or inspire the other to participation in some plan or hope.

These scenes are *agons,* moments of struggle, contests in which one of the characters is trying to prevail over the other. The implication in the politics of *Nostromo* is that the public order is the sum of private struggles in which noble motives are slogans to hide personal desires. That is why the irony of Captain Mitchell's narrative of the events leading to the creation of the Occidental Republic is so complete. He deals with the actions, but the reader knows motives. (That narration itself is an example of this structure by conversations. It deals with incredible events and for one, stupefying, seventeen-page day the reader is the captive of Captain Mitchell even more than is the fictitious tourist whom the Captain wishes to impress with the history of the glorious revolution and his role in it.)

One scene that reveals much of what the novel is about is between Martin Decoud and Antonia Avellanos; the love scene in the middle of the revolution which occupies half of the fifth chapter in Part Two, a chapter on which Ford Madox Ford had worked for Conrad. The lovers have returned to the Casa Gould after seeing off General Barrios on his expedition to crush Montero. (No small part of Conrad's irony, or grasp of reality, in his demonstration in the novel of the worthlessness of elaborate plans—such as that for crushing Montero or for saving the silver. Pure chance,

stupidity, and madness determine more events.) The leading citizens of Sulaco are assembling in the Gould salon to
consider ways of dealing with the revolution. Martin Decoud, editor of the *Porvenir* and vilifier of the rebel Montero,
has really come, however, to woo Antonia. Since she will be
won only by the champion of a noble cause, Decoud has
become a leader of the counterrevolution, despite his awareness that "he was not a patriot, but a lover."

As the crowd begins to gather, Antonia and Martin retreat
to one of the large windows where, partly shielded by a thick
curtain, they stand side by side looking down upon the Calle
de la Constitucion in one of the intensely private scenes of
which this public novel is composed. Charles and Emilia
Gould are the center of the group they have left and the pairs
of lovers are a mute commentary on each other. Both loves
will be destroyed by the idea of the mine and the noble
country its wealth is supposed to produce, and each love will
have, in the woman, a living monument in that noble, post-
revolutionary state. The women, Emilia and Antonia, come
to resemble the Intended in their devotion to the ideal of
what they imagined their men were.

While the distinguished citizens debate a course of action,
the lovers try to make their arrangements. Antonia makes
her private feelings for Martin and her father serve her devotion to her country; Martin, the *boulevardier*, consecrates
his passion on the altar of patriotism, saying:

"I have no patriotic illusions. I have only the supreme illusion of a lover."

He paused, then muttered almost inaudibly, "That can
lead one very far, though."

Behind their backs the political tide that once in every
twenty-four hours set with a strong flood through the Gould
drawing room could be heard, rising higher in a hum of
voices.

Decoud will be drowned in that political tide because he
acts out what he does not believe to get what he wants. To

those passing in the street it is "improper" for Martin and
Antonia to be standing thus together. Conrad takes the trouble to insist on just how improper their behavior is by repeat-
ing the reference three times. The real impropriety is not a
matter of mores. Both Antonia and Martin are dealing in
illusions and both act as if they can easily blend their public
and private desires. No union comes from their talk, however; only the separation of Sulaco. But Antonia does have
some satisfaction. She can live for the memory of her dead
hero, cherishing, like the Intended, the lie of his martyrdom.

Nostromo, as much as Decoud, is a victim of his illusions.
Conrad said, in a late letter, that silver, not Nostromo, is the
hero of the novel. Whoever or whatever is the hero, Nostromo's vanity is the core of the novel; the incorruptible
metal has value only to corruptible humanity.

Nostromo's sin is the Biblical sin of vanity, the sin which
afflicts all of the characters in the book. This vanity I take to
mean aspiration without regard to consequences, a sense of
the importance of self beyond the order of the cosmos, living
as if one were already a legend. Pride as Milton knew it, or
hubris, are other terms that might be used, but the Biblical
vanity has more the sense of self-anointing which is the characteristic sin in "the paradise of snakes."

Nostromo's tragedy is that of misplaced and ill-considered
idealism. He was meant to be a warrior-hero, but a progressive commercial state has little room for warrior-heroes. Like
Othello, he is a creature of enormous vanity and limited intelligence who has hired out his strength to the merchants.
His ideal of himself is the peasant counterpart of Gould's
sense of mission. Nostromo is not a refined intellect like
Gould dedicated to an idea; he is concretely and biologically
the "king of Sulaco," but he is afraid of the Northerners and
afraid to rule.

In a famous passage in the novel, after he has left Decoud
alone on the island with the silver, Nostromo awakens like
another Adam:

At last the conflagration of sea and sky, lying embraced and asleep in a flaming contract upon the edge of the world, went out. The red sparks in the water vanished, together with the stains of blood in the black mantle draping the sombre head of the Placid Gulf; and a sudden breeze sprang up and died out after rustling heavily the growth of bushes on the ruined earthwork of the fort. Nostromo woke up from a fourteen-hours' sleep and arose full length from his lair in the long grass. He stood knee-deep among the whispering undulations of the green blades, with the lost air of a man born into the world. Handsome, robust, and supple, he threw back his head, flung his arms open, and stretched himself with a slow twist of the waist and a leisurely growling yawn of white teeth; as natural and free from evil in the moment of waking as a magnificent and unconscious wild beast. Then, in the suddenly steadied glance fixed upon nothing from under a forced frown, appeared the man.

This Adam has already fallen. The forced frown represents his awareness of responsibility, his fear of failure, his memory of having been born into a world in which forces stronger than he imagined use him for their ends. He is killed by his only worthy adversary in the book, the Garibaldino, old Viola, another man with a sense of honor and no awareness of reality.

Nostromo is, like Decoud, a victim of his vanity; but he is also, like Hirsch, a victim of the technological progress of Sulaco. When we see him dodging the tramcars, we know he is doomed because the warrior-hero cannot survive in a world of tramcars and tight suits. He becomes as nervous, unsure, and self-conscious as the skipper in *The Secret Sharer*. In the end, this is what becomes of the capataz de cargadores, "The crew of his own schooner were to be feared as if they had been spies upon their dreaded captain." But it is the lighthouse that dooms him.

The lighthouse is a civilized, commercial creation meant to tame the darkness of the gulf. The light in the darkness is a link with *Heart of Darkness:* Kurtz speaks of such a beacon as a moral light. Nostromo also leaves behind him an intended, faithful to the memory of what he never really was. Kurtz and Nostromo are victims of their vanity which never allowed them simply to be human. They are victims of a naive idealism that either redeems a time or destroys a man.

Two hundred and thirty-nine years before Conrad finished his long struggle with *Nostromo*, Milton completed *Paradise Lost*. That epic of the beginning of modernism has a scene in which the fallen angels set about gouging precious metals from the bowels of Hell. What Holroyd and Gould do not realize is that while they work in the best modern way for a purer form of Christianity and a just state, they are, in fact, about the devil's business, serving a passion for this world which corrupts all of their idealism. Their tragedy is that they are genuinely committed to their ideals and do not realize how much they, the plutocrats, the great manipulators of others, are acting out a scenario prepared for them before the beginning of time:

> There stood a hill not far whose grisly top
> Belched fire and rolling smoke; the rest entire
> Shone with a glossy scurf, undoubted sign
> That in his womb was hid metallic ore,
> The work of sulphur. Thither winged with speed
> A numerous brigade hastened: as when bands
> Of pioneers with spade and pick axe armed
> Forerun the royal camp, to trench a field
> Or cast a rampart. Mammon led them on,
> Mammon, the least erected Spirit that fell
> From heaven, for even in heaven his looks and thoughts
> Were always downward bent, admiring more
> The riches of heaven's pavement, trodden gold,
> Than aught divine or holy else enjoyed

In vision beatific. By him first
Men also, and by his suggestion taught,
Ransacked the centre, and with impious hands
Rifled the bowels of their mother earth
For treasures better hid. Soon had his crew
Opened into the hill a spacious wound
And digged out ribs of gold. Let none admire
That riches grow in hell; that soil may best
Deserve the precious bane. And here let those
Who boast in mortal things, and wondering tell
Of Babel, and the works of Memphian kings,
Learn how their greatest monuments of fame,
And strength and art are easily outdone
By spirits reprobate, and in an hour
What in an age they with incessant toil
And hands innumerable scarce perform.

Milton used the Bible for his retelling of the creation of
the world. Conrad used it for his telling of the creation of a
state. Both are very concerned with sin. Milton's Biblical
epic is a mirror of its age, the time of the making of the modern
world in the era of Protestantism, capitalism, and individual-
ism. Conrad's political epic is, like Dostoyevsky's, an anti-
Gospel. Nostromo's real name, for example, is Giovanni Bat-
tista Fidanza: John the Baptist, the Faithful One. This John
the Baptist, however, is the precursor of Gould and of Holroyd's purer form of Christianity; he makes straight the path
of the Material Interests. Conrad's anti-Gospel is his effort to
show how man justifies his ways to Mammon. He looked to
Panama and saw the role of power and money in the creation
of a state. His anti-Gospel was meant to reveal the truth beneath the pious platitudes. He seems in this to have been
very like Dostoyevsky; fusing the private story of the sinner,
Nostromo, with the public story of a revolution, the purchase
of freedom for Panama.

Closer in time to Conrad's novel is D. H. Lawrence's deeply
felt portrait of the miner in *The Rainbow:*

"It is with the women as with us," he [Tom Brangwen] re-
plied. "Her husband was John Smith, loader. We reckoned
him as a loader, he reckoned himself as a loader, and so she
knew he represented his job. Marriage and home is a little
side-show. The women know it right enough, and take it for
what it's worth. One man or another, it doesn't matter all the
world. The pit matters. Round the pit there will always be
the side-shows, plenty of 'em."

He looked round at the red chaos, the rigid, amorphous
confusion of Wiggiston.

"Every man his own little side-show, his home, but the pit
owns every man. The women have what is left. What's left
of this man, or what is left of that—it doesn't matter alto-
gether. The pit takes all that really matters."

Many would be shocked at the linking of Charles Gould,
the director of the San Tomé mine, the King of Sulaco, with
a collier named John Smith. Emilia Gould would understand.

Mrs. Gould knew the history of the San Tomé mine. Worked
in the early days mostly by means of lashes on the backs of
slaves, its yield had been paid for in its own weight of human
bones. Whole tribes of Indians had perished in the exploitation; and then the mine was abandoned, since with this
primitive method it had ceased to make a profitable return no
matter how many corpses were thrown into its maw.

The mine, the pit, is a maw. The collier and the manager
are both in bondage to the mine. The collier is a slave to his
wage, but the man who keeps slaves to fulfill his vision becomes the slave of those slaves. So Charles Gould spending
the night away from his wife, up at the mine, acts out his
special bondage to his ideal.

The unprofitable mine devouring whole tribes of Indians
is an echo of the grove of death in *Heart of Darkness*. In
Nostromo, however, the mine is made to work efficiently and
profitably, the idea is realized. In this world, missionaries like
Father Corbelàn are more successful: "Rumors of legendary
proportions told of his successes as a missionary beyond the

eye of Christian men. He had baptized whole nations of Indians, living with them like a savage himself. It was related that the padre used to ride with his Indians for days, half naked, carrying a bullock-hide shield, and, no doubt, a long lance, too—who knows?" But Father Corbelàn, unlike Kurtz, comes back from the wilderness to become a Cardinal. Commerce and Christianity are, in *Nostromo*, triumphant, not as in *Heart of Darkness*, betrayed.

Emilia Gould is married to Charles; she is not his intended. She knows all that he does. She sees her beloved's dream, told her in the passion of their betrothal, of making the mine a "moral success" carried to its fruition. In that moment of joy, with an unconscious Miltonic note, she sees him as splendidly disobedient. To the end, with no conscious irony, she refers to him habitually as her "boy."

Nostromo completes *Heart of Darkness* by dealing with the triumph of the idea. That triumph is the source of Emilia's bitter consolation of Giselle, "Console yourself, child. Very soon he would have forgotten you for his treasure."

———◆———

Because the novel is so complex, a critic encounters a form of the Heisenberg principle in trying to discuss it: to arrest the flow of the action in order to analyze is to distort that which is to be analyzed. This, of course, is true of any work of literary art but is especially true in this novel of total irony for which the linear prose of criticism is no match for the contrapuntal poetry of the book. For this reason, among others, I think that one of the best commentaries on *Nostromo* is a poem: William Butler Yeats' "Easter 1916."

Yeats' poem is about men and women who try to create a country, and it captures all the confusions attendant on any human effort to bring about the reign of justice. Yeats knew that the creation of a nation, like the creation of a work of

art, required tremendous sacrifice. He also knew that too
much sacrifice can turn the believer's heart to stone and that
death, compromise, and betrayal are the probable rewards.
Yeats and Conrad both knew that the private self is the price
of public deeds and that when men and women act in the
name of an ultimate national good, then a "terrible beauty is
born."

Nostromo has its own terrible beauty. Conrad saw politics
as both impersonal economic forces and individual personal
morality. He saw politics as tragic mythology. In two works
at the turn of this century, Conrad made that mythology his
special subject. The ledger and the cross were its symbols
and Conrad asked of it, "What doth it profit a man?"

Imperialism is the name that history gives to this special
mythology. The two novels that deal with the human agents
of that myth end with lies. In Conrad's dark vision of our
world, this is the price of politics.

Chapter Six

Kafka: The Political Machine

IN THE PENAL COLONY is Franz Kafka's artistic statement of his sense of self-torture and the fantasies of self-destruction with which he lived. The story is also a prophecy of the horrors of German National Socialism in Europe from 1933 to 1945. The two visions, personal and public, psychological and political are, in fact, one.

The two are united because Kafka attempted no prophecy. He wrote of his own nightmare feelings so completely and so honestly that he wrote the history of the future when others made those feelings of guilt and self-torture motives for public policy and the nightmare became everyday reality.

If nazism had not happened, the story would still have mattered because it deals uniquely with the sense of pain with which some people somehow manage to live on a day-to-day basis. Nazism, however, revealed how that sense of the world as a torture chamber could be externalized and all the self-hatred redirected at the scapegoats. Nazism was a harnessing of the madness within and that is why it worked. Kafka is the poet of the madness within. Like Dostoyevsky, whom he knew, and Conrad, whom he did not, he wrote of the "Underground"—the dark cellar of unexpressed emotion wherein are stored the savage impulses of our lives. The modern artist has taken great pains to remind us that no social or political amelioration has removed those dark places. Hitler, himself a kind of daemonic artist, was able to reach within and tap them in his audience.

A terrible discovery that came in the wake of twentieth-century tyranny is the way in which ordinary men cooperated with it. The whole horror of nazism is unthinkable without the picture of some solid citizen in a small town thrilled to act at the Führer's command. What Kafka knew and wrote about before it had happened was the action of that good burgher. He knew that actions came from the tyranny of madness present in almost all of us and that Hitler in his person and his party suddenly made the madness acceptable behavior and released the ordinary man to act out the idea of torture he carried within himself.

The experiments of Stanley Milgram, reported in his *Obedience to Authority*, demonstrated that a large percentage of "normal" people will act in a brutal manner in a "totalitarian" situation. These people will excuse themselves on the grounds that they are acting in accordance with orders and with the requirements of authority rather than with simple humanity. The people become, in effect, automata; trapped in their own instinctive fears, unable to respond in a human way, they become what Kafka's Czech contemporary, Karel Capek, called "robots."

The robot is potential within the "normal" person. Kafka, knowing this, created in the character of the officer the symbol for the modern political robot. The Officer of *In the Penal Colony* is the character with whom we identify and he haunts us when the story is over. In fact, when Kafka toyed with new endings for the story, he had the Officer appear as a ghost on the ship with the Explorer. The character grips us as he does because Kafka writes the story from his point of view. As the focus of the action, the Officer speaks what Kafka feels and he appeals to us, represented by the Explorer, to understand him.

A doctrinaire Marxist critic of Kafka thought he detected a proto-Fascist streak in the novelist. He was on the right track but reached the wrong conclusion. We do not identify with the Officer because Kafka is a proto-Fascist; we identify with his capacity for devotion to that which will destroy him and recognize with a shudder that we understand his appeal because we share his madness. In writing of his own fear, Kafka could not have known that the Old Commandant would return and reverse, if only temporarily, the process of the gradual evolution of a benevolent state.

I do not think *In the Penal Colony* is a consistent allegory of any kind nor that there is a key to its meaning. Without attempting a systematic allegorical reading, I want to trace some of the relationships of the private and the public, the psychological and the historical, in the story. I will begin with the story itself and its sources and analogues in Kafka's fears, dreams, visions, and fantasies. That is its private dimension. The public I will consider in terms of Albert Speer's remarkable book, *Inside the Third Reich*. This memoir shows that Kafka did not write exclusively of feelings unique to him, nor of concerns solely theological. He wrote of human attitudes, and Speer reveals with terrifying ingenuousness how those attitudes made the Nazi holocaust possible. Finally, I want to talk about the point at which the private vision and the public prophecy meet: the technocracy, the country of technology and bureaucracy which is the modern state. Kafka's daily life was that of a bureaucrat and, as Heinz Politzer points out, "the highly technical description of the execution machine owes many a turn of phrase to the professional work Kafka had to perform for the Workers' Accident Insurance Institute. Ironically, one of his special fields of study was the prevention of accidents." This man, a bureaucrat crushed and sustained by the bureaucracy, the artist of the apparatus, a Czech Jew writing in German, alienated from his family and unable to make one of his own, haunted always by nightmares of torture, destruction and punishment,

wrote of his experience as the alien-citizen of the modern
state.

———————◆———————

In the Penal Colony opens with the Officer introducing the
Explorer to the machine—a remarkable apparatus. The opening in the hot, sandy valley with the two characters and the
mute chorus of soldier and condemned man seems to be that
of a story about Dreyfus on Devil's Island and Kafka's awareness of the Jew in the world of the imperial military. Typical
of Kafka, however, that expectation is set up in the reader
only to be frustrated. The real thread of the narrative begins
with the Explorer's indifference to the world and work of the
Officer. It is clear that the Explorer has come only to be
polite, and at the suggestion of the Commandant that he
might wish to witness the execution of a soldier for disobedience and insulting behavior. Because the story is so elusive,
I will retell it as simply as possible here.

The Officer is working very hard to interest the Explorer,
and somehow his exertions, in his heavy uniform, in the heat,
begin to disturb us. We are, at first, touched by the Officer's
anxiety that nothing go wrong. The Officer says: "Things
sometimes go wrong of course; I hope that nothing goes
wrong today, but we have to allow for the possibility. The
machinery should go on working continuously for twelve
hours. But if anything does go wrong it will only be some
small matter that can be set right at once." Only later do we
begin to realize some of the meaning in the Officer's pettish
remarks about the New Commandant—that he cannot disrupt
the design of the Old Commandant for the colony. It is
quickly evident that both apparatus and colony have fallen
far from their original designs.

The Explorer begins to be impressed by the Officer's hard
work in the heat. He, like the reader, begins to respond to the
enthusiasm of the other, an enthusiasm which seems attrac-

tive in the atmosphere of decay and lassitude. Such is the beginning of moral confusion: one begins by admiring enthusiasm until it becomes fanaticism, and even after that if it promises relief from boredom or the self. Kafka has begun involving us in the fate of the madman. When the Officer then begins his dramatic monologue of justification, the Explorer is already half-caught in the procedure; he "felt a dawning interest in the apparatus."

The Officer seems upset that the New Commandant has not explained to the Explorer how the sentence is to be executed. Yet, even as he condemns this latest breach of protocol, the Officer is pleased to be able to show to the visitor the plans and drawings for the machine, the scriptures of the Old Commandant. To the Explorer's surprised question as to whether the Old Commandant did everything, the Officer, with a glassy look, replies simply, "Yes." These scriptures, the elaborate plans for the machine are, according to Heinz Politzer, very like Kafka's own manuscript writings. In this sense the story is a statement by Kafka of his feelings about himself as a writer. His offense is to feel and see as he does; his punishment is to write what he feels with his own blood.

The Officer explains to the Explorer that, as the machine works, whatever commandment the prisoner has disobeyed is written into his body. In this case the statement is, "Honor Thy Superiors!" When the Explorer asks if the condemned man knows his sentence, the Officer replies that he will learn it on his body. When the Explorer expresses his shock at this, the Officer impatiently replies, "Guilt is never to be doubted." The offense of which the man is guilty is sleeping on duty and insulting a superior. The condemned man was required to get up at every hour to salute the door of his captain; and when at two o'clock in the morning the captain found him asleep and whipped him across the face, the man grabbed his foot and threatened to eat him alive. Now he is in chains and will be punished.

The offense is obviously one which fascinates Kafka. Among Karl Rossman's many misadventures in *Amerika* is his problem with the Head Porter who scolds him and judges him a troublemaker because Karl failed to greet him "properly" every time they met, no matter how many times, in the course of a day. The offense, in both works, seems an echo of some expected ritual acknowledgment of dependency within the family and the violation of the commandment to honor one's father and mother, but especially one's father.

The condemned man stands, therefore, in chains, waiting to be punished for his disobedience. The chains seem superfluous since we have already been told that he would probably not run away even if he were unchained. When Kafka wrote this story, it would seem logical to assume that readers would account for the passivity of the prisoner by his ignorance of his fate. History has made his attitude more ambiguous. He may be motivated by ignorance of his fate or he may be the victim who simply refuses to believe what is being done to him right up to the moment he is placed in the execution chamber. He may even, in his ignorance, blindness, hope, belief in the sanctity of his own life, guilt, or innocence, be a victim willing to be punished for whatever crime the authority says he has committed.

To the troubled Explorer, the Officer explains more of the details of the machine, pressing him to read the "script," the plan for punishment; but the Explorer cannot. Remarking that the calligraphy is not for school children, the Officer explains that the script is designed to be completed in twelve hours of writing. The implication of the remark about the calligraphy, coupled with the place of children at the grand executions in the old days, is that a child witnesses the torture of individuals in the world and then grows up to understand and to appreciate the elaborate mechanisms of torture humans have devised for themselves.

The Officer presses on with details of the machine's operation and speaks reverently of the sixth hour when the prisoner understands his sentence, "Enlightenment comes to the most dull-witted." This, says the Officer, was "a moment that might tempt one to get under the Harrow oneself." In the last six hours, relieved of the burden of doubt about his guilt, the prisoner grows in his understanding of his sentence until he dies.

Such, at least, is the plan of the Old Commandant and his disciple for bringing a citizen to awareness. The real operation is much less edifying. As the real prisoner is placed upon the machine, one of the wrist straps, which has rotted, breaks. The Explorer begins to question the whole operation but is not yet able to do anything. The Officer complains bitterly that the New Commandant is not supporting properly the execution machine. The Explorer, now concerned, wonders if he should intervene. He thinks it a ticklish matter for him, a visitor to the colony, not even a citizen of the mother country, and yet he wonders what he should do because, "The injustice of the procedure and the inhumanity of the execution were undeniable." The Explorer is, I think, giving the response of Cain. "Am I my brother's keeper?" is the first and the still unanswered political question.

The Explorer's uncomfortable thoughts are interrupted by the Officer's cry of rage. The condemned man vomited when forced to take the felt gag into his mouth. The Officer is furious because the machine is befouled. The New Commandant is at fault because he has not forced the prisoner to fast and his ladies have stuffed the prisoner with candy, "He has lived on stinking fish his whole life long and now he has to eat sugar candy!" The gag has not been replaced even though hundreds have chewed it and slobbered over it in their death agonies. The emotional logic of this disgusting scene seems to favor the Officer against the New Commandant. If the punishment is inevitable, if it is to be rammed down one's throat, then it is worse if it is sugar coated. I do not know if the Old and New Commandants correspond to the God of the Old and New Testaments, or, more personally, to Kafka's

grandfather, the butcher, and father, the dealer in ladies'
linens; but as the Officer himself later performs the ambiguous sexual gesture of accepting the gag into his mouth, he is
accepting the reality of pain and guilt which handkerchiefs
and candy cannot hide.

At this point the rhythm of the story changes; the Officer
asks to speak to the Explorer in "confidence." "This procedure
and method of execution, which you are now having the op-
portunity to admire, has at the moment no longer any open
adherents in our colony. I am its sole advocate." The Officer
has begun his direct appeal to the Explorer with a story of the
way it was in the old days under the Old Commandant when
hundreds turned out to witness the magnificent spectacle of
justice being done and jockeyed for seats close enough to observe in detail the transformation at the sixth hour. The Old
Commandant, in his wisdom, provided that the children
should have the preferred places from which to observe the
"look of transfiguration" so that, presumably, they would be
prepared, in their turn, to administer and to accept such justice. The Officer regrets that things have declined to the
point of no crowds and the filthy gag and that "it is impossible to make those days credible now."

As the Explorer looks away, the Officer mistakes his reaction for sympathy and asks if he does indeed realize the
shame of things as they now are. The Officer says that the
Explorer has been sent as a witness by the New Commandant so that he can discredit the whole procedure, but the
Officer pleads for his understanding and support. The Explorer is pleased to know that he can be influential and says
to the Officer, "I can neither help nor hinder you." Thinking
that he can get away that easily is part of the Explorer's
problem.

The Officer presses on, his mad paranoia becoming absolutely clear as he constructs a scenario for the next day's conference in which the Explorer can support him. The Officer is
planning a coup, an insane political gesture, like Hitler's in

1923, and he is demanding the Explorer's support: "it will force him [the New Commandant] to his knees to make the acknowledgment: Old Commandant, I humble myself before you. That is my plan; will you help me to carry it out?" The Explorer, even though "fundamentally honorable and un-afraid," hesitates for one breath, "No," he says, "I do not approve. . . . your sincere conviction has touched me, even though it cannot influence my judgment."

The Explorer hesitates because he is partially captured by the Officer's desperation. The Officer seems so pathetic, so human, so alive in the midst of the desolation, that we, the Explorer and the reader, have to respond to him. The Explorer is like Marlow and the Officer like Kurtz, the two conscious characters in the heart of darkness. In the midst of the banality around them, Marlow and the Explorer can understand and even be tempted by the nightmare vision of the man they find in the wilderness. The Explorer, the visitor to the penal colony, begins to feel the reality of guilt, and the barbarism always possible to man.

"So you did not find the procedure convincing," says the Officer, ". . . then the time has come." Because he has failed to convince the Explorer of the justice of his cause, the Officer is willing to sacrifice himself to that cause. As the condemned man is set free, the Officer presents another drawing to the Explorer and deciphers it for him when he cannot read the inscription: BE JUST. The soldier and condemned man cavort; the Officer wipes off the machine, strips naked, and throws his clothes into the pit. "The Explorer bit his lip and said nothing. He knew very well what was going to happen, but he had no right to obstruct the Officer in anything. If the judicial procedure which the Officer cherished were really so near its end—possibly as a result of his own intervention, as to which he felt himself pledged—then the Officer was doing the right thing; in his place the Explorer would not have acted otherwise." Confirmed in his policy of nonintervention, the Explorer assumes that self-destruction is not a form of

injustice or inhumanity. Perhaps he feels that it is necessary
to execute the primitive self, if the enlightened self is to rule
unchallenged.

The reactions of the condemned man are less self-conscious.
When the condemned man realizes that the Officer plans to
submit himself to the machine, he is happy: "So this was revenge. Although he himself had not suffered to the end, he
was to be revenged to the end. A broad, silent grin now appeared on his face and stayed there all the rest of the time."

The Officer places himself upon the machine and even is
able to take the gag into his mouth. The condemned man and
the soldier run up; the Officer allows himself to be strapped
in; the machine starts itself and works very quietly.

Then, as the Explorer and the other two watch, the machine goes crazy and begins to vomit out its insides. "The
explorer wanted to do something . . . to bring the whole
machine to a standstill, for this was no exquisite torture such
as the officer desired, this was plain murder." To the enlightened onlooker, the slow, exquisite torture of a life in pain
is acceptable, but the violence of suicide is not. The Explorer pushes the corpse of the Officer off the machine into
the pit. There is no change in the Officer's face, no sign of
redemption, only the great iron spike, like that on top of a
helmet, protruding through his forehead.

The story now becomes the story of the Explorer's reaction.
With the other two witnesses, he rushes from the scene to the
inhabited colony, to civilization. On the outskirts of the
settlement he stops at the teahouse in which the Old Commandant is buried. The building is old, dark and cavernous,
like a church, or a womb, or the dark places of the human
heart, and in it the Explorer "felt the power of past days."
The soldier tells him that the Old Commandant is buried here
because the priest would not let him lie in the churchyard.
The Explorer finds the grave against the back wall where the
poor people, the dock workers, are gathered. On the grave is
this inscription, "Here rests the Old Commandant. His adherents, who now must be nameless, have dug this grave and

set up this stone. There is a prophecy that after a certain number of years the Commandant will rise again and lead his adherents from this house to recover the colony. Have faith and wait!" Like Frederick Barbarossa, he may return.

The inscription seems a prediction of the horrors to come because Kafka saw so clearly into one kind of human psyche that he understood how it might express itself in history. We can now read the story as if it were a retrospective study of nazism; as if Kafka had seen it all, the concentration camps in which his sisters died, the torture machines, the ordinary men become fanatics, and simply recorded it. History gives the story its peculiar quality of *deja vu* and makes the inscription on the tomb of the Old Commandant seem a parody of the epitaph of Arthur of Britain: *Rex quondam et futuris.* In Kafka's story, the Old Commandant lies underground, in the cellar, the rat hole in the floorboards of civilization first described by Dostoyevsky's man with the diseased liver.

The habitués of the teahouse reveal nothing. They seem to find the inscription "ridiculous." The Explorer gives them some coins and leaves for the harbor. He gets away in a small boat and, when the soldier and the condemned man rush to the dock to join him in his flight to freedom, he threatens them with a knotted rope and makes his escape without them. This representative of the advanced, civilized, and rational nations wants no further business with the inhabitants of the penal colony. The Explorer wants nothing more to do with the darkness and destruction to which his explorations have led him. He will, if necessary, resort to force to keep himself free from involvement with anyone connected with the hideous act. He would lie if he were ever to meet the Officer's fiance back in the mother country.

———◆———

One of Kafka's most famous diary entries is that for August 2, 1914: "Germany has declared war on Russia.—Swimming in the afternoon." Just before this, in the entry for July 31 in which he mentions the General Mobilization, Kafka wrote: "But I will write in spite of everything, absolutely; it is my struggle for self-preservation." Dedicated to his writing and his private vision, Kafka seems to ignore the ordinary details of the outside world. What he does is to make his painful compositions stand for his sense of the realities of that world. Thus, *The Great Wall of China* is a parable of Kafka's vision of World War I and his status as a Czech, Jew, German in that war.

Kafka's political insight begins with his sense of himself as a victim of tyranny, the tyranny of his father: "For me you took on the enigmatic quality that all tyrants have whose rights are based on their person and not on reason. At least so it seemed to me." (*Letter to His Father*) He writes, later in the same letter, "My writing was all about you; all I did there, after all, was to bemoan what I could not bemoan upon your breast. It was an intentionally long-drawn-out leave-taking from you, yet, although it was enforced by you, it did take its course in the direction determined by me." Kafka, in that struggle, articulated his ambivalent feelings about that tyranny in such a way that the corpus of his work may be read as the statement of the individual as cooperative victim and willing prisoner in the process of destruction. The Officer makes clearer our responses to Erkel in *The Possessed* and to Albert Speer, the Nazi armaments minister who seems completely a Kafka character. We do not sympathize with what the Officer represents; we simply understand better the mechanisms of madness in the individual which can become the mechanisms of madness in the state.

Kafka's personal writings are filled with analogues to the machinery and the punishments of *In the Penal Colony*. His diary entry for July 21, 1913, reads: "This block and tackle of the inner being. A small lever is somewhere secretly released, one is hardly aware of it at first, and at once the whole apparatus is in motion. Subject to an incomprehensible power, as the watch seems subject to time, it creaks here and there, and all the chains clank down their prescribed path one after the other."

Later, on January 24, 1914, the year of the war and the story, Kafka made this entry in his diary: "Recently, when I got out of the elevator at my usual hour, it occurred to me that my life, whose days more and more repeat themselves down to the smallest detail, resembles that punishment in which each pupil must according to his offense write down the same meaningless (in repetition, at least) sentence ten times, a hundred times or even oftener; except that in my case the punishment is given me with only this limitation: 'as many times as you can stand it.'"

Still later, a few years after the publication of *In the Penal Colony,* in one of the *Letters to Milena,* Kafka writes and draws as follows:

So that you can see something of my "occupations", I'm enclosing a drawing. These are four poles, through the two middle ones are driven rods to which the hands of the

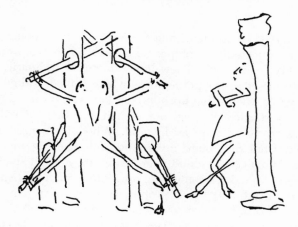

"delinquent" are fastened; through the two outer poles rods are driven for the feet. After the man has been bound in this way the rods are drawn slowly outwards until the man is torn apart in the middle. Against the post the inventor who, with crossed arms and legs, is giving himself great airs, as though the whole thing were his original invention, whereas he has only copied the butcher who stretches the disembowelled pig in his shop-front.

The torture machine, the *Apparat* mentioned over and over again in the beginning of the story, is part of Kafka's perception of everyday reality. Kafka is not the Officer any more than Dostoyevsky is the Underground Man, but the character is some part of the creator, and the Explorer speaks for Kafka's sane self in recognizing the inevitable self-destruction of the mad self. Kafka was not a "proto-Fascist;" his prophecy of nazism came from the fact that he wrote so clearly, so honestly of his own inner sense of destructive madness. He could not know that he spoke for a world.

The story seems not to have relieved Kafka of his terrible anxiety. The letter to Milena with its drawing is some years later, and the dream detailed below is recounted in the diary for January 1915, some months after the completion of the story.

I had agreed to go picnicking Sunday with two friends, but quite unexpectedly slept past the hour when we were to meet. My friends, who knew how punctual I ordinarily am, were surprised, came to the house where I lived, waited outside awhile, then came upstairs and knocked on my door. I was very startled, jumped out of bed and thought only of getting ready as soon as I could. When I emerged fully dressed from my room, my friends fell back in manifest alarm. "What's that behind your head?" they cried. Since my awakening I had felt something preventing me from bending back my head, and I now groped for it with my hand. My friends, who had grown somewhat calmer, had just shouted "Be careful, don't hurt yourself!" when my hand closed behind my head on the hilt of a sword. My friends came closer, examined me, led me back to the mirror in my room and stripped me to the waist. A large, ancient knight's sword with a cross-shaped handle was buried to the hilt in my back, but the blade had been driven with such incredible precision between my skin and flesh that it had caused no injury. Nor was there a wound at the spot on my neck where the sword had penetrated; my friends assured me that there was an opening large enough to admit the blade, but dry and showing no trace of blood. And when my friends now stood on chairs and slowly, inch by inch, drew out the sword, I did not bleed, and the opening on my neck closed until no mark was left save a scarcely discernible slit. "Here is your sword," laughed my friends, and gave it to me. I hefted it in my two hands; it was a splendid weapon, Crusaders might have used it.

Who tolerates this gadding about of ancient knights in dreams, irresponsibly brandishing their swords, stabbing innocent sleepers who are saved from serious injury only because the weapons in all likelihood glance off living bodies, and also because there are faithful friends knocking at the door, prepared to come to their assistance?

In August 1917, Kafka began to work on alternate endings for *In the Penal Colony*. He had said of the story, after reading it aloud at Franz Werfel's, that he was "not entirely dissatisfied, except for its glaring and ineradicable faults." Whether or not the remark was simply ironic, Kafka did continue to think about the ending of the story. The diary entries for August 7, 8 and 9, 1917, have to do with changes in the story—changes that were never made. Most revealing in connection with these contemplated changes, however, is the entry for August 3, 1917, where Kafka records a dream in which he is one of his own characters: "Once more I screamed at the top of my voice into the world. Then they shoved a gag into my mouth, tied my hands and feet and blindfolded me. I was rolled back and forth a number of times, I was set upright and knocked down again, this too several times, they jerked at my legs so that I jumped with pain; they let me lie quietly for a moment, but then, taking me by surprise, stabbed deep into me with something sharp, here and there, at random." Having dreamed his story, Kafka toyed with end-

ings in which the ghost of the Officer haunts the Explorer
who thinks he can get away.

Kafka made the Officer so moving and so persuasive because he lived his fate. He wrote, as he said, as an act of self-
preservation. Thanks to that we can understand better some
of the madness of modern history.

◆

A bureaucrat concerned with technology, driven to write
his nightmares, is a possible description of Franz Kafka. *In
the Penal Colony* is, among other things, a symbolic treatment of the two most important "facts" of modern political
life: technology and bureaucracy. The two "facts," unideo-
logical and apolitical, shape the citizen's experience of the
state. Apparatus and system are not the causes of the modern
state, but its products. The connection between Kafka's story
and nazism is that the Nazis made the nightmare real. The
Nazis used the products of the modern state to bring about
the rule of barbarism. One of the best commentaries on this
dimension of *In the Penal Colony* is *Inside the Third Reich*,
the memoirs of Albert Speer.

Speer was an architect who became, early in the 1930's,
Hitler's personal architect and city planner. Always close to
Hitler, hard-working and talented, he became in 1942 Minister of Armaments and War Production and devoted himself
to organizing the German economy for the prosecution of the
war. At Nuremberg he was sentenced to twenty years in
prison and, while serving his sentence at Spandau, wrote his
reflections on Hitler, on himself, on the technocracy of evil
he served so well. As he says, in his strange mixture of confession and defense, of denunciation and apologia, "Dazzled
by the possibilities of technology, I devoted crucial years of
my life to serving it." One can open Speer's memoirs at random and come upon passages that are eerily Kafkaesque.
This, for example, is how the Minister of Armaments and War

Production speaks of his accomplishments in the service of a regime he now knows to have been completely evil:

> Within half a year after my taking office we had significantly increased production in all the areas within our scope. Production in August 1942, according to the *Index Figures for German Armaments End-Products*, as compared with the February production, had increased by 27 percent for guns, by 25 percent for tanks, while ammunition production almost doubled, rising 97 percent. The total productivity in armaments increased by 59.6 percent. [footnote omitted] Obviously we had mobilized reserves that had hitherto lain fallow.

The prideful rhetoric seems familiar because it is the rhetoric of the Officer trying to convince the Explorer of the efficacy of the system and the apparatus.

In another passage, Speer includes, unknowingly, the guard and the prisoner. The only difference is that these are real people, prisoners of war:

> The prisoners themselves, as I sometimes had a chance to observe, also feared Himmler's growing economic ambitions. I recall a tour through the Linz steelworks in the summer of 1944 where prisoners were moving about freely among the other workers. They stood at the machines in the lofty workshops, served as helpers to trained workers, and talked unconstrainedly with the free workers. It was not the SS but army soldiers who were guarding them. When we came upon a group of twenty Russians, I had the interpreter ask them whether they were satisfied with their treatment. They made gestures of passionate assent. Their appearance confirmed what they said. In contrast to the people in the caves of the Central Works, who were obviously wasting away, these prisoners were well fed. And when I asked them, just to make conversation, whether they would prefer to return to the regular camp, they gave a start of fright. Their faces expressed purest horror.
>
> But I asked no further questions. Why should I have done so; their expressions told me everything. If I were to try today to probe the feelings that stirred me then, if across the

span of a lifetime I attempt to analyze what I really felt—
pity, irritation, embarrassment, or indignation—it seems to
me that the desperate race with time, my obsessional fixation
on production and output statistics, blurred all considera-
tions and feelings of humanity. An American historian has
said of me that I loved machines more than people. [footnote
omitted] He is not wrong. I realize that the sight of suffering
people influenced only my emotions, but not my conduct. On
the plane of feelings only sentimentality emerged; in the
realm of decisions, on the other hand, I continued to be
ruled by the principles of utility. In the Nuremberg Trial the
indictment against me was based on the use of prisoners in
the armaments factories.

By the court's standard of judgment, which was purely
numerical, my guilt would have been greater had I prevailed
over Himmler and raised the number of prisoners in our
labor force, thus increasing the chances of more people for
survival. Paradoxically, I would feel better today if in this
sense I had been guiltier. But what preys on my mind nowa-
days has little to do with the standards of Nuremberg nor the
figures on lives I saved or might have saved. For in either
case I was moving within the system. What disturbs me more
is that I failed to read the physiognomy of the regime mir-
rored in the faces of those prisoners—the regime whose existence I was so obsessively trying to prolong during those
weeks and months. I did not see any moral ground outside
the system where I should have taken my stand. And sometimes I ask myself who this young man really was, this young
man who has now become so alien to me, who walked
through the workshops of the Linz steelworks or descended
into the caverns of the Central Works twenty-five years ago.

A final quotation from Speer should make clear Kafka's
political significance.

In a sense my hopes had been realized. The judicial guilt had
been concentrated to a large extent upon us, the defendants.
But during that accursed era, a factor in addition to human
depravity had entered history, the factor that distinguished
our tyranny from all historical precedents, and a factor that

would inevitably increase in importance in the future. As the top representative of a technocracy which had without compunction used all its know-how in an assault on humanity, [footnote omitted] I tried not only to confess but also to understand what had happened. In my final speech I said:

> Hitler's dictatorship was the first dictatorship of an industrial state in this age of modern technology, a dictatorship which employed to perfection the instruments of technology to dominate its own people. . . . By means of such instruments of technology as the radio and public-address systems, eighty million persons could be made subject to the will of one individual. Telephone, teletype, and radio made it possible to transmit the commands of the highest levels directly to the lowest organs where because of their high authority they were executed uncritically. Thus many offices and squads received their evil commands in this direct manner. The instruments of technology made it possible to maintain a close watch over all citizens and to keep criminal operations shrouded in a high degree of secrecy. To the outsider this state apparatus may look like the seemingly wild tangle of cables in a telephone exchange; but like such an exchange it could be directed by a single will. Dictatorships of the past needed assistants of high quality in the lower ranks of the leadership also—men who could think and act independently. The authoritarian system in the age of technology can do without such men. The means of communication alone enable it to mechanize the work of the lower leadership. Thus the type of uncritical receiver of orders is created.

The *Penal Colony* and the *Third Reich* are the same place. Such is the power of Kafka's vision that he writes in 1914, not as if terrible potentialities will be realized, but as if they already had been.

In the penal colony the inhabitants are exiles and emigrés, the disenfranchised citizens, those in exile in the country of their birth. At the heart of the chronicle of this colony is the machine that renders justice. To have **BE JUST** tatooed into the body is a parody of the teaching of political virtue, a basic responsibility of the state. In *The Republic* Socrates tried to define justice by describing the just state and its citizens. Plato wrote of a state of which justice was the soul. Kafka envisioned a state in which the *Apparat* was the soul.

In the Penal Colony was written in 1914, the year of Armageddon, the beginning of the end of the modern era. Kafka wrote before the advent of the totalitarian state, but he wrote as one who had seen it and returned. Thirty years later, other, less visionary men travelled to that strange country. All subsequent statistics and reports tend to verify the accuracy of Kafka's preliminary sketch.

Chapter Seven

Mann: Art, Politics, and the Apocalypse

THE NOVEL WITH WHICH to compare *Doctor Faustus* is the other great tragedy of tyranny written in America, *Moby Dick*. Both books are celebrations and damnations of the extraordinary man, the possessed man who will, if he must, destroy all human relationships in the realization of his dream.

Adrian and Ahab, Serenus and Starbuck are the characters who act out the drama of citizen and ruler, unique talent and ordinary virtue, decent quiet and destructive achievement, while we, the spectators at the great political and artistic events of the modern world, look on in uneasy fascination.

Both *Moby Dick* and *Doctor Faustus* center on a pact with the devil. Ahab consecrates his harpoons and says, "I baptize thee *in nomine diaboli.*" The crew of the Pequod becomes an extension of himself. Adrian, having made his pact with the devil, loves Echo, his nephew-son, and touches him. But the devil is destruction and the man infected by the demon will spread the infection until it destroys the innocent ones who voyage with him. The novels are strange and equivocal celebrations of these men who make pacts with the devil. The books are haunting because they deal with the fascination of the tyrant, the man who destroys but offers some insight into a God-challenging mind, into the Promethean spirit by which humankind created itself. Both books, nurtured in the homeland of democracy, are tortured hymns to the powers of the tyrant.

Ahab and Adrian: each is the Man-Artist-Tyrant-Trickster-Hypnotist who lives only to accomplish his aim, to make real his vision, to prevail by strength of will in a world of small desires. The artist and the tyrant are in this alike: each will realize his sense of what might be, regardless of the cost to himself or others. Ahab and Adrian, blood brothers, could stand for either Adolf Hitler or James Joyce: for that titanic arrogance by which some unique creation will be thrust upon the world. Hitler and Joyce, roughly contemporaries, redefined the possibilities of inherited forms—the state and the novel—and both used parody as their means, the madman inadvertently, the artist intentionally. Ahab and Adrian are their fictional counterparts; the tyrant and the artist driven to make their wills prevail over the intractable material given them by nature and history.

Because both books have an explicit concern for creation, destruction, and the true nature of the sensible world, each has a specifically religious element. In *Moby Dick* there is Father Mapple's sermon on Jonah and the whale. (Jonah is one of the marked men, one of the outsiders, one of the "chosen ones," who figure again and again in the works of Melville and Mann.) In *Doctor Faustus*, in roughly the same place in the narrative, Adrian is exposed to the theological lectures of Ehrenfried Kumpf and Eberhard Schleppfuss at the university at Halle. The novels, in effect, create the religious tradition against which their Promethean protagonists will rebel.

The analogues in the two novels come from the complementary vision of their creators. Both are deeply influenced by Shakespeare. Ahab's cadences derive from Melville's annotated copy of the plays, read just before he began his masterpiece. Adrian adapts *Love's Labours' Lost* and sees himself as the negation of Prospero, as the black against the white magician. It is as if both artists wanted their works to be measured against other, comprehensive visions of the soul of man. Melville challenges Shakespeare and the Book of Job. Adrian says that he will "take back" Beethoven's Ninth Symphony. Mann, at the same time, is invoking Marlowe, Goethe, and Shakespeare to challenge the meaning of creation in the literature of his native and his adopted land.

Ahab's story and Adrian's require a narrator. Serenus Zeitblom is like Starbuck in his fundamental, orthodox decency, but he is also like Ishmael, the spectator who survives to tell the tale. Like Marlow in *Heart of Darkness* and Govorov, the narrator of *The Possessed,* the ordinary man is our necessary witness to the truth of the extraordinary tales that are told. It is almost as if Melville and Mann use their narrators to shield us from the direct, destructive force of their protagonists.

The use of the narrators points to another relationship between *Moby Dick* and *Doctor Faustus:* their approach to the epistemological problem of modern fiction, the problem of the truth of the narrative. Reading these books is wrestling with material that seems left over from notebooks and technical manuals, and Mann indulges his inclination to pedantry by creating characters who lecture. In *Moby Dick* there are facts of whaling; in *Doctor Faustus,* facts of music. The novelists want to convince us of the reality of their subjects by their circumstantial attention to the facts of a process. It is as if they did not trust their medium to convey the full reality of their vision of the horror and so ground it in the factual to prove that it is real.

The modern world and the first two Fausts, that of the chapbook and Marlowe's, are products of the Renaissance. The epistemological problem is another. What does the mind know and how does it know it? Two answers created to an-

swer Montaigne's question—*Que sais-je*—are science and the
novel, two forms for knowing, describing, evaluating, and
responding to the world present to the senses. For some
novelists, Melville and Mann in particular, the epistemological problem is part of the novel itself: what kind of
"truth" does art contain; what is the "reality" in the realistic?

In their greatest novels, this problem appears in the distrust of eloquence. Both novelists shun it, smother it, and try
to deny it, until it finally breaks through all the notation designed to restrain it and the author is involved in the celebration in prose of a monster. Mann and Melville are concerned
with the fate of one man who is raised above the ordinary by
his dedication to a quest and who, in living out his doom,
destroys others. All the feelings of the reader, however ambivalent, are caught up in the fate of the protagonists and for
the duration of the voyage or the composition, we wish him
to reach his goal, to have the confrontation with the universe
that he seeks.

———◆———

Throughout his long creative life, Thomas Mann was
troubled by his sense of himself as an artist. He seems to
have been haunted by the idea that the artist is the mountebank, the trickster, the confidence man that the solid burgh-
ers think he is. Mann knew that the poet shared with Cipolla,
the *artiste* in *Mario and the Magician*, the desire to mesmerize his audience; he always seemed uncertain about
whether the vocation to mesmerize exempted the performer
from the moral sanctions that applied to his audience. Mann
never doubted the importance of artistic creation in the life
of mankind; what he tried again and again to determine was
the real price of that creation, to the artist and to his audience.

One way in which Mann tried to fix the price and value of

art was in relation to politics. In three works that span nearly a half-century of creative work and the political experience of the first half of the twentieth century, Mann dealt with the relation of art and politics. First is the short story, "Gladius Dei" (1902); then the novella, *Mario and the Magician* (1929); *Doctor Faustus* (1947) is the culmination of Mann's tragic fiction in two ways: it is his summary statement of the problem of the artist, and of the destiny of man in the twentieth century which, he said, would be decided in political terms.

A critic has said that modern writers write longer and longer books about nothing. In other words, because there is no body of shared beliefs in artist and audience, the artist starts with nothing and must create the context and then the book about the context. Whether the observation is true or not, it has some relevance to Mann's work. Mann profoundly distrusted art and was never sure what the artist is and, therefore, he created a vast corpus of work to explore the question of whether art is trustworthy. In particular political terms, Mann was concerned with whether Hitler was what he called him in an essay of uneasy irony entitled "A Brother": an artist? Was he an artist as spellbinder and a mountebank like Cipolla and, if so, was he different in kind or merely in degree from Thomas Mann, Nobel Prize winner? Mann wrote and rewrote his portraits of the artist to overcome his own distrust of what he was doing. In *Doctor Faustus* especially, he gives the narration of the story to the clumsy and pedantic Serenus so that it will not be too artistic. He did not want his story of the artist to be too "captivating" because it was also the story of the artist who had captivated a nation into its ruin. Mann struggled throughout his life with the part of him that was Adrian and the part that was Serenus and the very different values of art which they represent. His two early re-creations of Savanarola are the beginnings of his artistic awareness of politics.

In *Fiorenza* (1904), his play on the clash of Savanarola and

Lorenzo de Medici, Mann allows an expression of his distrust of art in conventional terms: art squanders goods needed to relieve the sufferings of the poor, the social argument of *The Princess Casamassima*. This expression is, however, like the motives assigned to Iago in *Othello*, perfectly plausible and perfectly inadequate. The real feelings transcend rational motives. Mann's distrust of art and his worship of art are so profound that no statement of social conscience is adequate to the dual vision from which he works. Savanarola, Mussolini and Hitler; Hieronymous, Cipolla and Adrian: for good or ill, only the fanatic is comparable to the artist.

As much as anything else, the setting of "Gladius Dei" convinces me of the accuracy of Pound's statement that artists are the antennae of the race and Lewis's dictum that the artist writes the history of the future. "Gladius Dei" is set in Munich, the "radiant" and "tolerant" city. Into this city comes Hieronymous, the fanatic armored in his beliefs. Reading now about the man and the city causes a shiver of recognition: this was the city of Hitler's Beer Hall Putsch and the conference that gave us peace in our time. Perhaps the city was too radiant and too tolerant.

In "Gladius Dei," Munich is synonymous with corruption because its values are derivative and its aesthetic concerns have no moral counterparts. Munich was to Mann the southern city to which he came after the death of his father and the failure of the family business in the burgher north. The city of art was chosen by his mother, but Mann, the young artist, saw himself as a stern outsider, a serious northerner in a frivolous southern city. Mann wrote in 1923 to Felix Bertaux, the French translator of *Death in Venice* who had asked for biographical details, "I have never really felt spiritually at home in Munich, to which my brothers and sisters and I were transplanted when I was barely out of boyhood." So strong were Mann's feelings about Munich, in fact, that more than forty years later, in *Doctor Faustus,* he writes of Inez Rodde, "Inez at bottom despised the aesthetic traffic of the

sense-loving city into which she had been transplanted by
her mother's craving for a less strait-laced life."

Mann felt himself, in his serious devotion to art, more like
Hieronymous than the pandering owner of the emporium of
beauty, Herr Blüthenzweig. Mann wrote the history of the
future of Munich by writing honestly about his feelings in
the present; like Kafka and Yeats, he realized that autobiog-
raphy is history and projected into the story his own sense of
the absolute and intolerant demands of real art in a tolerant
and derivative world. Because Mann sees himself in this way,
he is ambivalent in rendering the character of Hieronymous,
the destructive fanatic. To put it simply, Mann makes us feel
far more sympathetic toward the intolerant critic of easy art
and loose morals than we are to all the other, nonfanatical
characters in the story. That ambivalence remains through
Mann's maturity and appears again, more marked, more profound and more disturbing, in his portrait of the artist as
fanatic, Adrian Leverkühn.

The sentence "Munich was radiant" is repated at the
beginning and end of the first movement of "Gladius Dei."
The repetition has a musical quality which always interested
Mann: the presentation, development, and return, with
changes, of a dominant theme. The repetition also frames the
city and, like a boundary, marks off a small world in which
the only values are aesthetic. "Decorative" is probably a better word than "aesthetic" because art in radiant Munich has
no serious content: it is the embellishment but not the transformation of the ordinary. All manner of art and near-art
forms appear in this first movement, but they are lush and
overdone and give a sense of the saturation of artifice in all
the activities of the city. The young men, for example, stroll
from the library, whistling the *Nothung* motif, with "literary
periodicals" stuffed in their pockets. The premise underlying
the elaborate presentation is that when the aesthetic crowds
out all other standards of judgment, art itself becomes derivative and false. The opening statement that the city is "radi-

ant" seems to contradict the ominous title and to lead, in the glory of the June day, to a celebration. The second reference to the city's radiance is ominous and disturbing; it anticipates the flames and lightning with which the story closes.

The center of radiant Munich is the artists' quarter where there is no cutthroat commercial competition. The center of this quarter is the Odeonsplatz with its loggia, the Feldherrnhalle, modeled on the Loggia dei Lanzi in Florence. Into this world strides the fanatic Hieronymous. In contrast to the plump natives, the gaunt Hieronymous stands for others of that name: for Hieronymous Ferrarensis, known to history as Girolamo Savanarola; for Hieronymous Bosch, another northern artist with a very different sense of art from that of the coyly pretty southern city; for St. Jerome, artist, believer and misogynist, who translated the words of God into spare Latin because the ornate would be a blasphemous distraction from the sacred message.

Mann's brief story concerns the clash of Hieronymous with the values of radiant Munich. With characteristic irony, Mann forces the reader to identify with the puritan reformer, and the reader is then in the uncomfortable position of supporting the enemy of tolerance and art.

Hieronymous, clad as a monk, enters the city and strides to the church to make his visit. Unlike the crowded sidewalk in front of Herr Blüthenzweig's window, the church is occupied only by one crippled woman. The church is the place of refuge for the grotesque—for Christ crucified—and the deformed woman has no place in the city of art. The crippled woman is in silent contrast to the two young girls who giggle and run when they see Hieronymous. In the church, in a clear sexual reference, Hieronymous grows larger and grasps himself more closely. He has the basic marks of the true fanatic: distorted sexuality and an inner conviction of the rightness of his vision.

As Hieronymous leaves the church, he is drawn to the crowd in front of the art shop where another madonna is being worshipped on her altar in the window. This madonna, a sepia photograph of a painting, nude and beautiful, holds a figure of the Christ-child who plays with her breast while he glances knowingly at the spectator. As he stares at the picture, Hieronymous overhears two students discussing the "facts" of the case: the madonna is the painter's mistress, the painting has insured the artist's success and he has already dined twice with the Prince Regent. The students leave, agreeing to meet later at a performance of Machiavelli's *Mandragola,* while Hieronymous continues to stare at the madonna, an elaborate copy of a blasphemous joke which insured the artist's success.

Hieronymous finally turns away, but he is haunted by the picture and on the third day he receives a summons from his God to bear witness against this "insolent cult of beauty," this celebration of the sensual. Pleading at first that he is an unworthy instrument, Hieronymous finally yields and goes, reluctantly, to do the Lord's bidding.

The day is sultry and a storm is brewing as Hieronymous, muttering, "It is God's will," enters Herr Blüthenzweig's establishment. The interior of the shop is a miniature of the city. There is a choking abundance of art, of "color, line and form, of style, wit, taste and beauty." In this hothouse of *objets d'art* are three customers: a gentleman with a black goatee in a yellow suit "bleating" over a portfolio of French drawings, an elderly lady examining embroidered flowers, and an Englishman handling a bronze statuette, a provocative nude of a young girl. The proprietor, Herr Blüthenzweig, is selling that statuette assiduously. At 150 marks he says it is "An example of Munich art, sir." The city of art, free from commercial competition, is a city that panders to foreigners.

A customer enters quickly and buys a bust of Piero de Medici, the son of Lorenzo the Magnificent, and this Florentine touch sets the stage for the confrontation of Hieronymous and Herr Blüthenzweig. The Englishman takes the nude girl and is accompanied to the door with much bowing and scraping by the proprietor. Herr Blüthenzweig then turns to Hieronymous who says that he wishes to speak to him about the picture of the madonna. Blüthenzweig interrupts to assure him, with great professional confidence, that the excellent reproduction costs only 70 marks. Since, however, we have just seen Blüthenzweig act the pimp, the phrase is a *double entendre:* the lady is for sale, for whatever purposes, and if the gentleman says that he is an art lover, no questions are asked. The goateed man in the yellow suit continues to bleat over the portfolio of French drawings.

Hieronymous demands that Blüthenzweig remove the picture from the window and never exhibit it again because it is the Holy Mother of God. Hieronymous never makes clear whether it is the subject, the picture itself, or both to which he objects. He seems, however, to hate the sensual indulgence which masks itself as art and in so doing he represents a part of Thomas Mann who distrusted all his life the temptations to soft anarchy represented by the celebration of the senses.

Blüthenzweig, knowing that he is not dealing with a paying customer, calls his assistants to get rid of Hieronymous. They are like the two young men whom Hieronymous overheard on his first day in Munich, the young men who said that the picture made them doubt the doctrine of the Immaculate Conception. One of them says to Hieronymous that the picture is a work of art "and as such it must be judged by the appropriate standards." Hieronymous replies that the picture was painted in "sensual lust." He asks, "what impulses beget beauty, and to what does it appeal?" He assumes that unless it is redeemed by submission to the religious, the aesthetic is the realm of Satan. The assumption is close to that of Adrian Leverkühn who likes the idea of music submissive to a liturgy and who also has a bad experience in the art world of Munich.

In the emotional logic of the story, Hieronymous seems nearer the truth than the gigglers and panderers with whom he comes in contact. His peroration is powerful:

Art is the sacred torch that must shed its merciful light into
all life's terrible depths, into every shameful and sorrowful
abyss; art is the divine flame that must set fire to the world,
until the world with all its infamy and anguish burns and
melts away in redeeming compassion.

He sounds very like that other fanatical believer—Kurtz—and
in the world of decadent mediocrities in which their passions
burn, it is Kurtz and Hieronymous in whom we want to believe in spite of what we know about their precious "compassion."

Hieronymous now gives himself up to his madness, scream-
ing at Blüthenzweig that he must burn everything because it
is all filth. Blüthenzweig summons Krauthuber, the packer,
from the back room and this huge, dumb, "son of the people"
throws Hieronymous into the street. Krauthuber, the hench-
man, symbolic even in name, socially, economically, and in-
tellectually represents the ugly, brute force beneath the
world of gilt-edged editions and magnificent reproductions.

Hieronymous, staggered, in the street, sees in his "mad
ecstasy" the shop and the whole city burning and sees, in a
bolt of lightning in the gathering storm, the radiant sword of
God and the fire of judgment.

Hieronymous's final, reiterated "Burn" is an ironic reference to the fate of the Savanarola he represents. The identification with the Florentine and with St. Jerome, the passionate
and learned puritan, and with Bosch, the artist of the divine
grotesque, alters the reader's response to his undignified
fate. History quickly validated Mann's treatment of Munich
in a way he could not have imagined. The Savanarola figure
foreshadows Hitler, another fanatic who rose from the streets
of Munich to condemn the decadence of his country, to de-
mand blood instead of artifice, and to call for the burning of
the wicked books. Like Savanarola he, too, would finish on
the pyre he ignited. By writing so carefully of his own ambivalent feelings about art and its cult of sensual beauty, of
the artist, his freedom, and responsibility, and of his own
northern reactions to his mother's southern city, Mann is able

to identify some of the complex forces which shaped subsequent history.

In another sense, the corrupt aesthetics of Munich foreshadow the corrupt aesthetics of nazism with its torchlight processions and mammoth spectacles. Decadence and fanaticism are, like race prejudice, false aesthetics, perversions of the ideal of physical beauty about which Serenus Zeitblom is to speak. Beneath the surface, waiting to be shaped or manipulated, is the brute force of Krauthuber. Mann struggled all his life to define an aesthetic ideal that was not perverse and with the idea that the aesthetic ideal of redeemed nature is itself an illusion, the trick of the confidence man upon his gullible public. He embodied that struggle and his doubts in great works of art.

Mann, the artist, makes us admire Hieronymous, the fanatic opponent of art, because Mann deals directly with the problem of art as a medium for re-creating and evaluating human experience. The nagging question, for which Matthew Arnold did not stay for an answer, is whether the aesthetic is a sufficient category for the evaluation of the moral and the political. For the representation of them, the answer is clearly yes; but Mann questions the appropriateness of art in its representations to engage in the evaluation of moral and political realities. Since art must do this, if it is to be art and not merely decoration, the paradox can only be stated and restated and never solved.

The question is as old as the banishment of the poets from *The Republic*. The theme of "Gladius Dei" is the relation of art to piety. Plato reluctantly banishes the poets on moral-political grounds; they disturb the equilibrium of the commonwealth. Mann uses art to redeem art and creates sympathy for the moral fanatic because he is the only person in the story to give to art the serious attention it deserves. Plato and Hieronymous share the conviction that art is a significant human concern and, if it is severed from morality, it becomes trivial, corrupted, and corrupting. Mann realized in 1902 that a world in which art had become trivial was a world vulnerable to some kind of blood fanaticism. With an irony he lived to see and suffer from, history proved him right.

———◆———

Machiavelli, a younger contemporary of Savanarola, would probably have liked *Mario and the Magician*. It is set in a unified Italy and deals with power.

Mann gives his parable of power his mark: the tyrant is not a merchant prince but a performer, a conjurer who is both dictator and artist. The artist as conjurer is as old as Chaucer's Pardoner and Shakespeare's Prospero, but Mann makes his artist-conjurer one who captures and controls a political audience. Prospero is the tyrant of his island and the Pardoner is contemptuous of his audience, but Cipolla represents the sordid reality of dictatorship in a way the other characters do not. With the advance of liberal democracy in the nineteenth century, benevolent tyranny, no longer considered politically realistic, became a subject for nostalgia, a staple of science fiction and fantasy. The artist and conjurer who becomes a king is now a sinister figure.

Mann, the modern artist, bears the additional burden that he does not have the freedom of unself-conscious analogues of state and stage and must justify the act of creation in the process of creation. Chaucer's Pardoner is a gelding and his profession is to dazzle and deceive in the name of alleged spiritual benefits. He is available as a character for Chaucer to use. Shakespeare drew on the Medieval tradition of the *maître de jeu* and the *régisseur,* the on-stage director with wand and book for communal dramas, to create his tyrant-magician-poet-stage manager-director. Shakespeare could still present a man of total power and not worry about the political implications.

Mann's reflexive artists and performers are very self-conscious about their work and the pain of creation. Mann's artist stories, and those of every other modern writer, border on solipsism. In concentrating on the problems of the artist and using art—creation and performance—for plot, and the history of art—*Faust* and *The Odyssey*—as subject, the writer triumphs when he finds a way to show how art and the artist stand for important human experiences beyond themselves. This saves him from the trap of solipsism. Part of our fascination with literature is watching the artist work, like a matador, closer and closer to the horns. In "Gladius Dei," *Mario and the Magician,* and *Doctor Faustus*, Mann uses the idea of the artist as tyrant with greater and greater daring, taking greater and greater risks, to express his sense of the tragedy of the artist as the tragedy of modern man: the artist's private anguish stands for the public tragedy of politics.

In *Mario and the Magician*, Cipolla is *artiste* and tyrant; *Cipolla* means "onion" and the "onion" is Mussolini. Conjuring and controlling an audience from a stage becomes a metaphor for the basic political process, the exercise of power. In 1936 in the Preface to *Stories of Three Decades*, Mann wrote that *Mario and the Magician* was "a tale with moral and political implications." That modest phrase refers to the fact that Mann saw that the essence of the political process is dialectic and that the literary counterpart of dialectic is the *agon* of the drama. On that analogue Mann constructed his story.

The usual *agon* is that in which two characters contend with each other to bring about some change: Tiresias and Oedipus, Stavrogin and Peter Verkhovensky, Marlow and the Intended. Mann makes the central *agon* of his story that of Cipolla and his audience, the dramatic *agon* is a political dialectic and the symbol for the role of the tyrant in the remaking of a state.

Mann uses his theatrical metaphor to make a judgment on the political material he is presenting. The setting for this story of emergent fascism is a third-rate road show in a second-rate resort town. Cipolla, however, is an extraordinary performer. Mann, the man, hated the political phenomenon; but Mann, the artist, saw the inherently theatrical quality of facism: it is a shoddy vehicle with great opportunities for the star performer.

The confrontation of Cipolla and his audience is the center of the story, but that moment is prepared by all of the confrontations which precede it. The story is the sum of its confrontations as Mann embodies his "moral and political implications" in contending pairs of qualities: hospitality and barbarism; science and emotion; Nordic mind and Mediterranean heart; knowledge and superstition; comfort and discomfort; Torre di Venere and Portoclemente; homosexuality and heterosexuality; the childlike and the adult; real and make-believe; tragedy and farce; art and morality. All of these could be expressed as "versus" because the common theme is dialectic, the struggle for place and power.

In his book on Mann, Henry Hatfield complained that after Mann's remark about the moral and political implications of the story, readings of *Mario and the Magician* became "rigidly allegorical." But, Hatfield goes on, "the symbolism is not limited to the political realm; there is the philosophic as well: the struggle of free will against the forces of the occult and the subconscious." Those themes are in the story, but they represent the private experiences that are subsumed in the political. In fact, it was in the political realm that these forces emerged in Germany during the decade after the story appeared. The allegory would be too rigid if it represented only Italian fascism at a particular moment in time. Mann presents that phenomenon and evaluates it, but as an artist he concentrates on the timeless political process, the dialectic, and renders it in his dramatic *agons*.

As the story opens, the narrator we come to know so well but whose name we never learn, is still trying to comprehend what he has seen. He is fussy, almost simple-minded in his narration, a direct forebear of Serenus Zeitblom. The narrator and his family stand for Mann and his family and their experiences on a summer holiday in Italy in 1926. In creating the persona, the mask of a clumsy storyteller, Mann increases the verisimilitude of the story: no story told by such a solid, respectable, and unimaginative citizen could be anything but the truth. The reader understands more than the narrator and that, of course, is Mann's design.

> The atmosphere of Torre di Venere remains unpleasant in the memory. From the first moment the air of the place made us uneasy, we felt irritable, on edge; then at the end came the shocking business of Cipolla, that dreadful being who seemed to incorporate, in so fateful and so humanly impressive a way, all the peculiar evilness of the situation as a whole. Looking back, we had the feeling that the horrible end of the affair had been preordained and lay in the nature of things; that the children had to be present at it was an added impropriety, due to the false colours in which the weird creature presented himself. Luckily for them, they did not know where the comedy left off and the tragedy began; and we let them remain in their happy belief that the whole thing had been a play up till the end.

Because Cipolla is the tyrant in the same way that Oedipus is *tyrannos,* he incorporates "in so fateful and so humanly impressive a way, all the peculiar evilness of the situation as a whole." The dictator incorporates into himself all the evil latent in the body politic and then gives it back, as dividends, to the citizens. The children never know the difference between comedy and tragedy and, in the end, the reader is afraid that the narrator has not completely understood the nature of fascism. The cheap Punch and Judy quality of the performance and the childish element in the audience are all part of Mann's evaluation of the extremes of nationalist politics.

All of the omens are bad when the German family arrives in Torre di Venere. The visitors seem doubly strangers because the Italy they are visiting has changed so completely.

Hysterical reaction to the child's lingering cough sends the
family from their hotel to the Casa Eleonora, run by Signora
Angiolieri and her husband. She is the former travelling
companion of the great Duse and has named the pensione in
memory of that past affiliation. In the beginning of his story,
Mann characteristically joins the themes of sickness and art;
the child's infection is linked to the memory of Duse, a preparation of the combination of the sickness and hypnotic power
of Cipolla.

The children in the story, even in their relatively small
roles, are good indicators of political realities; they respond
instinctively to the melodrama of politics and they mimic the
attitudes of their elders. As their chidren are harassed on the
beach, therefore, the German visitors "gradually. . . realized
the political implications and understood that we were in the
presence of a national ideal. The beach, in fact, was alive
with patriotic children—a phenomenon as unnatural as it was
depressing. . . . There were quarrels over flags, disputes
about authority and precedence. Grown-ups joined in, not
so much to pacify as to render judgment and ennunciate principles." To the children made uncomfortable by the chauvi-
nism, their parents offer what consolation they can: "These
people, we told them, were just passing through a certain
stage, something rather like an illness, perhaps; not very
pleasant, but probably unavoidable." The condescension of
the narrator fits his character but is part of the worrisome
question of just what has he learned at the end of the story.
He thinks himself a superior, "scientific" German, able to rise
above this simple Italian hysteria. What the narrator sees,
however, as "passing through a stage," a sort of national
adolescence, is really a stage in the history of national evolution; and the German does not imagine what the next step,
for a more enlightened, less emotional, nation might be.

The *agons* on the beach stand for the process of power
with which the story is concerned, and the furor that erupts
when the child stands naked for a moment while she rinses

out her bathing suit stands for the insane mixture of nationalism, sexual perversion, and political corruption of the
small Italian town. Prudishness is the projection of a painful
or humiliating self-consciousness of sex upon another, and
the prudishness about the naked child is even more absurd
because the natives insist that the matter is *molto grave*. For
the offense to public decency a fine is assessed and contributed "to the economy of the Italian government." In this way,
in this now strange country, offenses against sexual morality
are made to profit the political order. The owners of the
Casa Eleonora, representatives of the old Italian style, provide some comfort for the visitors.

The assumptions of the German visitors that shape these
opening scenes in the hotel and on the beach are that Italians
are neither inhospitable nor prudish. The strange hostility,
the self-consciousness of these Italians, all the petty confrontations are to prepare the entrance of Cipolla. His performance
is the answer to the doubts and questions raised by the trivial
incidents in the hotel and on the beach, and even the unper-
ceptive narrator understands something of how Cipolla's performance—the bending of an audience to the hypnotic will of
an illusionist—accounts for the changes in a nation.

The narrator and his family do, however, aid in a small way
the final triumph of the dictator. Like ordinary citizens who
do nothing as the political climate changes because they do
not know what to do and are frightened by the fact of change
itself, the family ignores the unpleasantness and decides to
stay. "Shall we go away whenever life looks like turning in
the slightest uncanny, or not quite normal, or even rather
painful and mortifying? No surely not. Rather stay and look
matters in the face, brave them out; perhaps precisely in so
doing lies a lesson for us to learn. We stayed on and reaped
as the awful reward of our constancy the unholy and staggering experience with Cipolla."

The show itself, the culmination of the vacation visit, is
reached by a journey through history:

> The Cavaliere's performance was to take place in a hall
> where during the season there had been a cinema with a
> weekly programme. We had never been there. You reached
> it by following the main street under the wall of the "pa-
> lazzo," a ruin with a "FOR SALE" sign, that suggested a
> castle and had obviously been built in lordlier days. In the
> same street were the chemist, the hairdresser, and all the
> better shops; it led, so to speak, from the feudal past the
> bourgeois into the proletarian, for it ended off between two
> rows of poor fishing huts, where old women sat mending nets
> before the doors.

The stage is approached through time and class, and the
performance will consist of one man controlling and reshap-
ing the history and class allegiances of his audience.

The performance is incredible. Cavaliere Cipolla, *"forza-
tore, illusionista, prestidigatore,"* sick, twisted, and perverse,
captivates his audience in the same way that Chaucer's Pardoner dazzles the pilgrims. From the beginning, Cipolla's act
is an *agon,* a contest in which the reader is a spectator at the
struggle of Cipolla with the audience. Cipolla at first seems
only a mountebank, but very quickly the audience learns
that he is serious and that his "performance" is the imposi-
tion of his will upon them, upon Italy, and upon the world:
"We heard [in the audience before the performance starts]
English and German and the sort of French that Rumanians
speak with Italians."

The *giovanotto* who first challenges Cipolla and who represents simple strength and sexual virility is literally bent to
Cipolla's will. After that incident, all acts are bargains of
power between Cipolla with his whip and the audience.
Cipolla is the ruler of his subjects and the recipient of the
fascinated hatred of those who know themselves to be subjects. His "tricks" do not always turn out precisely right, but
this insignificant margin of human error makes his audience
identify with him even more strongly.

Mann makes very clear that his subject is dialectic and not

the command of robots by his description of Cipolla's quest
for the object hidden by the audience:

> The object passed from hand to hand which it was his
> task to find, with which he was to perform some action
> agreed upon beforehand. Then he would start to move
> zigzag through the hall, with his head thrown back and
> one hand outstretched, the other clasped in that of a guide
> who was in the secret but enjoined to keep himself per-
> fectly passive, with his thoughts directed upon the agreed
> goal. Cipolla moved with the bearing typical in these experi-
> ments: now groping upon a false start, now with a *quick*
> forward thrust, now pausing as though to listen and by
> sudden inspiration correcting his course. The roles seemed
> reversed, the stream of influence was moving in the con-
> trary direction, as the artist himself pointed out, in his cease-
> less flow of discourse. The suffering receptive, performing
> part was not his, the will he had before imposed on others
> was shut out, he acted in obedience to a voiceless common
> will which was in the air. But he made it perfectly clear
> that it all came to the same thing. The capacity for self-
> surrender, he said, for becoming a tool, for the most uncon-
> ditional and utter self-abnegation was but the reverse side
> of that other power to will and to command. Commanding
> and obeying formed together one single principle, one
> indissoluble unity; he who knew how to obey knew also
> how to command, and conversely; the one idea was com-
> prehended in one another. But that which was *done*, the
> highly exacting and exhausting performance, was in every
> case his, the leader's and mover's, in whom the will be-
> came obedience, the obedience will, whose person was the
> cradle and womb of both, and who thus suffered enormous
> hardship.

Cipolla acts out the will of his audience, finds the pin in
the shoe of an Englishwoman and presents it to Signora
Angiolieri. He cannot, however, bring himself to say the required sentence, "I present you with this in token of my respect," in French because this would violate his sense of

nationalism, but finally manages to say it in Italian with the last word in French. "And this partial success, after the complete success before it, the finding of the pin, the presentation of it on his knees to the right person—was almost more impressive than if he had got the sentence exactly right, and evoked bursts of admiring applause."

Cipolla's "act" is that of the dictator, the performer who compels his audience to follow and who sometimes leads by becoming what his audience most wants to be. This effort of will is staggering and drives Cipolla, again and again, to the cognac he uses like fuel. And, when the audience begins to feel sorry for a young man Cipolla has made rigid and balanced, head and feet, between two chairs, Cipolla mocks the feelings: *"Poor Soul!* . . . 'Ladies and gentlemen, you are barking up the wrong tree. *Sono io il poveretto.* I am the person who is suffering, I am the one to be pitied." Cipolla says that it is his expenditure of will which holds the man suspended. In a travesty of Michelangelo's lying on his back, exhausting himself in the execution of his vision, Cipolla spends himself in the performance of his "art."

In *Mario and the Magician,* Mann is actually putting the *Legend of the Grand Inquisitor* on the vaudeville stage. The Cavaliere, a perverse Don Juan, captivates Signora Angiolieri, a link with a nobler theatrical art, and forces her to come to him. Releasing her, unharmed, he warns her helpless husband that he must protect her because "there are powers stronger than reason and virtue." Cipolla sets members of the audience to dancing and these hostages of the group give themselves to "the drunken abdication of the critical spirit which had so long resisted the spell of this man." When one participant yields himself to Cipolla, the narrator, our witness, realizes, "He seemed quite content in his abject state, quite pleased to be relieved of the burden of voluntary choice." So troubled is the narrator that he is moved to a philosophical explanation of the illusionist's power, "If I understand what was going on, it was the negative character

of the young man's fighting position which was his undoing."
He is describing a Roman youth who valiantly resisted Cipolla's command to dance. "It is likely that *not* willing is not
a practicable state of mind; *not* to want to do something may
be in the long run a mental content impossible to subsist on.
Between not willing a certain thing and not willing at all—in
other words, yielding to another person's will—there may lie
too small a space for the idea of freedom to squeeze into."
Cipolla coaxes, "Is forcing yourself your idea of freedom?"
and the young man yields. The narrator concludes, "In a way,
it was consoling to see that he was having a better time than
he had had in the hour of his pride."

The triumph comes just before Cipolla's fall. Like his comic
counterpart, Chaucer's Pardoner, the spellbinder goes too
far and provokes a violent reaction. Even though that violent
end is anticipated in the first paragraph, it bursts upon us
with a sense of confused horror.

Mann was still hopeful in 1929. Mario's execution of
Cipolla and rejection of his bondage offers some hope, however ambiguous, for the strength of the human impulse to
freedom. But the comfort is scant. The actions can be sorted
out: the beckoning, the Roman salute, the kiss, the shot,
Mario's arrest; but the meaning for the narrator and the
reader is obscure. In forcing Mario to kiss him, the prestidigi-
tator and tyrant goes too far. Carried away by his own performance, Cipolla finally exceeds the limits of his audience.

Mario does not kill Cipolla because he has been ordered
to do something. At the intermission of the performance, the
narrator's children call out their usual command to him,
"*Mario, una cioccolata e biscotti!*" He answers with a smile,
"*Subito, signorini.*" Mario, the waiter, is used to taking orders,
but he cannot take humiliation. After the kiss, the mocking
laughter of the *giovannotto* makes Mario realize that he faces
daily humiliation and, driven mad, he kills the tyrant, the
source of his shame. His act will, ironically, incur the penal-

ties of the civilized order which tolerated Cipolla's performance.

The theme of freedom and bondage ends with Mario's act; the children care only to have stayed until the end, and the narrator experiences the pistol shot as a "liberation." The murder finishes both the public and private worlds of the story: Mario turns upon the tyrant when the tyrant ventures into his private world. The kiss is too much because it is a violation of the separation of the intimate and the obligatory, even for a citizen in a totalitarian state. Exposed and humiliated, Mario strikes back. (Most of the horror of modern totalitarian governments is, of course, the degree to which what is public and official intrudes upon and controls the intimate lives of its citizens.) All the themes of freedom and bondage, perversions personal and political, are present in that final, conclusive *agon* of Cipolla and Mario. They are a blur to the narrator because too much happens too fast for him to comprehend, and the rest of the citizenry waits for the next act.

In 1929, contemplating what he hoped was merely a "stage of development," Mann used a third-rate sideshow as a metaphor for political reality; but his solid burgher on holiday is so disturbed that he must convince his children, and himself, "that the whole thing had been a play up till the end." The story did not, however, drive the demons from the stage, and Mann was compelled to write a longer, more complex, and much more painful story of perverse art and political sickness. In 1929, the horror was real but still limited, and Mann could respond with what he hoped was art's saving irony and present Mussolini's fascism in the shoddy vaudeville of Cipolla.

Later, when the politics of insanity triumphed, Mann had to write more personally and stretch the limits of his fiction to try to present the German tragedy. For the horror of nazism, Mann sought his metaphors, not in the drama of

Duse, but in the philosophy of Nietzsche, the music of Beethoven, the poetry of Goethe and Shakespeare. These are the only adequate references for the aesthetic and moral history he had to write. That the greater political insanity demanded greater art is a terrible paradox for the humanist.

———◆———

Thomas Mann's career has a special relationship to the history of modern Germany. Born shortly after Germany became a unified nation, he saw his country become a European and a world power. He saw that nation go to war and be defeated. Then, in exile, he watched his country conquer Europe and rule on a scale that matched Hitler with Napoleon and Germany with the Roman Empire. When Mann died in 1955, Germany was again as it had been just before he was born: a divided country. He took upon himself the responsibility for giving artistic form to the grotesque triumph of German nationalism in the twentieth century. *Doctor Faustus* is the discharge of that burden; the artistic reflections of a political man.

Doctor Faustus is three stories. The first is the biography of Adrian Leverkühn, the modern artist willing to go as far as he must in order to be able to create; "the problem for the highly gifted artist was how, despite his always increasing fastidiousness, his spreading disgust, he could still keep within the limits of the possible."

Germany since Luther, especially Nazi Germany, is the subject of the second story in which Adrian's biography is a model for the history of the nation and the germ that entered the German mind with Luther and lay there until it produced Hitler and the Nazis, the national apocalypse. The question in this story concerns the limits of nationalism: Is what happened a uniquely German phenomenon or were the Germans simply the first to carry to a logical conclusion the meaning of the state of power?

Finally, *Doctor Faustus* is an exploration of the limits of art itself. Mann, most traditional of the titans of modern literature, distrusted art and dwelt upon its irrational and unhealthy qualities. As Serenus says, he distrusts the products of genius because "the daemonic and irrational have a disquieting share in this radiant sphere." In *Doctor Faustus*, Mann was concerned to see what a novel might contain.

All three concerns of *Doctor Faustus* are part of the great questions left unanswered at the creation of the modern world in the Renaissance, the time of the original Faust. For the person, the nation, and art are there any logical, aesthetic, or moral limits to human action, or must each idea be free to develop to whatever end it can? The Renaissance symbol for its break with the past was that of sailing beyond the pillars of Hercules to discover new worlds. One was the nation-state and another was the novel. *Doctor Faustus* asks us to consider the fate of both.

Mann controls the stories of *Doctor Faustus* and all their dimensions with a simple principle of structure. As "return" is the pattern of *The Possessed*, "echo" is the pattern of *Doctor Faustus*.

Mann was able, in *Doctor Faustus*, to make a musical pattern embody his narrative. He does it by having Serenus as a narrator. Since Serenus is not a novelist, he cannot tell the story in an artful way. Rather, he must break it down into its elements and recount them as best he can. The result is the creation of one of the most sophisticated novels of the twentieth century in the guise of a clumsily told biography. The self-conscious primitivism of the narrative is Mann's tribute to his complicated task: the exploration of the artist as tyrant and the meaning of German civilization in the face of the self-conscious barbarism of the Nazis. It is all done with echoes.

The beautiful child is only one of the echoes. His disease "echoes" that of his uncle-father and his name stands for the *ecce homo* of Adrian, Nietzsche, and Pilate. As he goes forward and backward in time, anticipating and recapitulating, Serenus makes a book of echoes. He, in fact, composes, because a musical composition is based upon controlled reverberations, precisely the kind of "unintentionally" controlled reverberations Serenus uses.

As part of the sophisticated primitivism of the book, Mann states explicitly the principle on which the novel is constructed, but has Serenus do it unconsciously. He does it in speaking of the young Adrian, the student of Wendell Kretschmar, precocious in the theory of harmony:

> In the schoolyard, between a Greek and a trigonometry class, leaning on the ledge of the glazed brick wall, he would talk to me about these magic diversions of his idle time: of the transformation of the horizontal interval into the chord, which occupied him as nothing else did; that is, of the horizontal into the vertical, the successive into the simultaneous. Simultaneity, he asserted, was here the primary element; for the note, with its more immediate and more distant harmonics, was a chord in itself, and the scale only the analytical unfolding of the chord into the horizontal row.

Later, in his room at Halle, Adrian has on the wall a magic square:

> On the wall above the piano was an arithmetical diagram fastened with drawing-pins, something he had found in a second-hand shop: a so-called magic square, such as appears also in Dürer's *Melancolia*, along with the hour-glass, the circle, the scale, the polyhedron, and other symbols. Here as there, the figure was divided into sixteen Arabic-numbered fields, in such a way that number one was in the right-hand lower corner, sixteen in the upper left; and the magic, or the oddity, simply consisted in the fact that the sum of these numerals, however you added them, straight down, crosswise, or diagonally, always came to thirty-four. What the principle was upon which this magic uniformity rested I never made out, but by virtue of the prominent place Adrian had given it over the piano, it always attracted the eye.

Finally, in the chapter just before Adrian's collapse, Serenus gives a detailed analysis of Adrian Leverkühn's last work, *Fausti Weheklage*, the Lamentation of Faust. Serenus sums up Adrian's triumph in this way:

> Here marshalled and employed are all the means of expression of that emancipatory epoch [of Monteverdi] of which I have already mentioned the echo-effect—especially suitable for a work wholly based on the variation- principle, and thus to some extent static, in which every transformation is itself already the echo of the previous one.

That last work, the Lamentation, is the completion of the magic square:

> Here I will remind the reader of a conversation I had with Adrian on a long-ago day, the day of his sister's wedding at Buchel, as we walked round the Cow Trough. He developed for me—under pressure of a headache—his idea of the "strict style," derived from the way in which, as in the lied "*O lieb Mädel, wie schlecht bist du,*" melody and harmony are determined by the permutation of a fundamental five-note motif, the symbolic letters h, e, a, e, e-flat. He showed me the "magic square" of a style of technique which yet developed the extreme of variety out of identical material and in which there is no longer anything unthematic, anything that could not prove itself to be a variation of an ever constant element. This style, this technique, he said, admitted no note, not one, which did not fulfill its thematic function in the whole structure—there was no longer any free note.

Echo, echo-effect, variation as echo, the magic square, the horizontal and the vertical simultaneously: these are the principles of Adrian's composition and of Mann's novel. The end result is a creation beyond freedom.

The echo-effect works within and beyond the novel. When Adrian collapses, Frau Schweigestill rushes to him and cradles him in her arms. This scene echoes that in which his mother, Elsbeth Leverkühn, holds Adrian's much younger head upon her breast because she is unwilling for him to go with

Kretschmar and give himself to music. Both scenes are echoes of the *Pieta*. As a young artist, Mann had repeated the sentence "Munich was radiant" to mark off a movement in a story. In *Doctor Faustus* Mann works with a mature musical pattern of announcement, development, and recapitulation, of controlled echoes.

It is the same technique which enables Mann to take details directly from the biography of Nietzsche and the music of Schönberg. Even more boldly than in the Joseph tetralogy he makes one character in the story stand for a line of historical characters. So the horizontal movement of the book is the biography of Adrian Leverkühn, composer. The vertical is all of German history from Luther to Hitler; and both horizontal and vertical echo each other. Artist and tyrant exist in Adrian and stand for the artist-tyrant relationship in German history: in Luther himself, in Beethoven and Goethe with Napoleon, in Thomas Mann and Hitler. As the Devil says to Adrian, "The artist is the brother of the criminal and the madman."

When, at the beginning of Chapter XXXIII, Serenus contrasts the time *in* which he writes with the time *of* which he writes, he is calling attention to the fivefold structure of the book: the time of Adrian Leverkühn; Germany in the twentieth century; Serenus writing in Germany about Adrian; Mann in America writing about himself through Serenus and Adrian; the mind of the hypothetical reader invoked at the beginning and ending of the narrative and its sense of the simultaneous present of the other four worlds. All is controlled in Mann's magic square. So controlled that the translator's small mistake about time (pages 421 and 425) is startling.

The most startling echoes in the book are those from Mann's own life and work. Besides quoting directly from one of his own stories, I think that, somewhere in *Doctor Faustus*, Mann alludes to every other work he had published. He makes the same free use of his own personal experiences.

Born a Gemini, Mann divides himself into Adrian Leverkühn and Serenus Zeitblom for his portrait of the artist as a German citizen. I believe that Serenus means exactly this when he says, "My subject is too close to me." "The life I am treating of was nearer to me, dearer, more moving than my own." Serenus is the public Thomas Mann; sober, conservative, an heir, as he says, of Reuchlin and the other Renaissance humanists. Adrian is the private Thomas Mann, the artist of the painful and the grotesque. I think Mann divided himself and used echoes because part of the penance for his country which he does in the book is to reveal details of his own life that are too painful for direct presentation but too important to be left out.

Clarissa Rodde is the daughter of the house in which Adrian was like a son, and the terrible details of her suicide by cyanide are an exact recording of those of Mann's sister's suicide. Inez Rodde's feelings about Munich, I have already quoted. The use of his own, living grandchild for vivid details of the tragic Echo indicates that Mann had the requisite degree of coldness for the "speculation of the elements" of life into art. Finally, it is his special obsession, the incest of brother and sister, which Mann uses in this book, as Dostoyevsky had used his obsession with child abuse in *The Possessed*, to represent the destructive emotions of his protagonist. Inez Rodde and Rudi Schwerdtfeger, the only man with whom Adrian is *per du*, are characterized repeatedly in their affair as being like a brother and sister who moved beyond familial affection to incest.

Echo is the child of Adrian's sister, born out of sequence from his much older brothers and sisters. He is the child of the sister whose wedding drove Adrian to a terrible migraine and the magic square of composition. The death of Echo, the human he wanted to love purely, drives Adrian to his greatest work. In the end, in his madness, he babbles that the child was his and that the devil had brought his sister as his bedmate. He is probably only speaking out his guilt at the death of the child.

In his last monologue, with its echoes of Faustus' last

speech, Adrian compares his bed-sister to the Little Mermaid of Hans Christian Andersen. In that grotesque story, filled with details too hideous for any form except a child's fairy tale, the mermaid trades her song for love. Adrian who has already gone to the bottom of the sea with "Professor Aker-cocke" has experienced her choice. He, the artist, may have love or song, but not both. If he is to create, it must be done in pain and involve the betrayal, if necessary, of everyone close to him.

In *Doctor Faustus*, the state is rendered in terms of the vision of the artist; art and tyranny are products of a vision in which nothing else matters except the realization of that vision. But if there can be no question of morality in artistic execution, how can art encompass and condemn a Hitler? Are the artist and tyrant so nearly akin that the artist must, as Blake said of Milton, be of the devil's party and celebrate energy itself?

Mann makes such questions vex Serenus Zeitblom. Serenus assures us in the beginning that he cannot write like a novelist, and Mann takes the risk of having Serenus demonstrate that fact. In a sense, Serenus is like Johan Conrad Beissel, the backwoods dictator, who rediscovers in his master and servants notes the elements of music. Mann is using Serenus ironically: only those capable of struggling through the book earn its revelations of the nature of tyranny and the nature of creativity.

In another sense, however, Serenus is seriously the human conscience of the artist which wants art to have a *paideiaic* function. For Serenus, art must be Apollonian; it must be capable of shaping values. For Adrian art is Dionysian, chthonic and disruptive; it is an escape from moral values into the transcendent discipline of form. The resolution of the novel, such that it is resolved, is that both are right: the artist consumes himself to make his vision real; the humanist tames that production to the collective ends of the community. The terror of the novel comes from the sense that the commanding vision is always daemonic and the humanist only buys time before the next eruption.

Serenus's complex feelings about Adrian reflect his creator's divided loyalties. How can Thomas Mann, German novelist, use his art to reveal the degradation of Germany? How can he not? If nazism is immortalized in art, might men not love it too much? When Serenus says, concerning the fate of his nation, that there is "something we fear more than German defeat, and that is German victory," he is summing up the artistic and political problem of the book. Can an artist be a traitor in his art; and if so, to what?

It is interesting to speculate on the works of the counter-exiles, Thomas Mann and Ezra Pound. One fled from fascism, the other moved to it. Each tried, by broadcast, to convince his countrymen at war that he was right and they were wrong. Each was deeply conservative, in the artistic sense, and believed that he acted from a higher allegiance than loyalty to an existing political regime. Mann seems to have made more significant art of his "treason" than did Pound.

Since he cannot make a tragedy of Nazi Germany, he makes a tragedy of his own divided sense of himself as an artist and a citizen. The echo principle extends to all of the doubles in the book: two dogs, two Rudis and two arts, literature and music, among so many others. The book itself has a double focus: time present and time past; two cultures, Renaissance and modern; two languages, English and German; two literary Fausts, two musical Fausts. All of these are part of the Apollonian-Dionysian split of narrator and hero in the novel. Mann makes his novel from his own tortured sense of the divisions in him and hopes, thereby, to exorcise his demons and Germany's.

The Faust story is the ideal vehicle for Mann's ambivalences. It belongs to his native language in the sixteenth-century chapbook and the Romantic epic; it belongs to the language of his adopted country in Marlowe's drama. In the Renaissance versions, Marlowe's and the Faustbook, the protagonist is damned; the overreacher is sent to Hell for his presumptuous bargain. In Goethe's epic, overreaching is the protagonist's salvation, and the image of unlimited extension of the self replaces the medieval vision of limits, circles, and a closed universe. Mann uses both themes. Serenus condemns the Nazis who embodied the idea of the unlimited extension of the self—the Führer—and the unlimited extension of the state. Adrian's creations, won at the price of going beyond previously determined limits, are Mann's expression of faith in the artist as overreacher. In his novel, Mann is able both to damn nazism to its flames and assume fully his role as the artist of that *Götterdammerung.*

Mann's nickname in his immediate family was *Der Zauber,* the magician. He deals in *Doctor Faustus,* as part of the doubleness of the book, with the two great magicians, experimeters and tyrants of Renaissance drama, Faust and Prospero. Representing the powers of black and white magic in the affairs of men, one uses his power to have more experience of himself; the other uses his to restore harmony to a world. Adrian, who begins with *Love's Labours' Lost,* finishes with *The Tempest.* Just before his collapse, having used Prospero's dismissal of Ariel as his epitaph for Echo, Adrian succumbs completely to the black magic and says that the artist is not the calm Prospero in contrast to the tortured Faust. The artist, Adrian says, is Caliban, the articulate beast.

The artist, as Mann made clear in the character of Cipolla, is both the master and the slave. He is slave to a vision which possesses him, demanding to be made manifest. He becomes then a tyrant and forces that vision on all around him, using them as Mann used his family, to make offerings to placate the daemonic demands. The artist and the tyrant, Faust, Luther, Beethoven, Napoleon, Cipolla, Adrian, Hitler, and Mann, derive their power from their single-minded devotion to that which they must do in order to live. As Adrian knows and Serenus does not want to admit, only in the complete surrender of the self to some other order can the full expression of the self be accomplished. The moral nature of the order does not matter to the expression. That is why there is no resolution of the problem, only the eternal struggle of Ariel and Caliban, Adrian and Beethoven.

———◆———

Like James Joyce, whose work he knew through Harry Levin's book and from whom he borrowed the idea of a catalogue of styles in the third part of Chapter XXXIV, Mann wanted a mythic frame for his unpromising subject. Like Joyce he wanted an epic form to sustain the serious parody he wanted to write. In Mann's case, the literary parody of the epic stands for the Nazi parody of national destiny.

Henry Hatfield identified parody as a constant in Mann's work, "*Tristan* is Mann's first parody, using the term, as he does, to mean the retelling of a myth from a modern, self-conscious point-of-view." By the time of *Doctor Faustus*, Mann is using parody as a frame for the story and for details. In the depiction of Fitelberg, the voluble booking-agent, he is parodying a parody: the character of Osric in Hamlet. Mann and Joyce are so serious in their parody because they feel it provides the freedom they need to create. As Serenus says, "In truth parody was here the proud expedient of a great gift threatened with sterility by a combination of scepticism, intellectual reserve, and a sense of the deadly extension of the kingdom of the banal."

When Adrian says, "Why does almost everything seem to me like its own parody? Why must I think that almost all, no, all the methods and conventions of art today *are good for parody only. . .* ?" he is articulating the problem of the modern artist, the problem Walter Jackson Bate has called "the burden of the past." Given his knowledge of all that has been achieved, how can an artist be creative, original, and

significant? One possible answer to the seemingly unanswer-
able question is radical parody. The artist can "take back" *Ode
to Joy, The Odyssey,* and *Faust.* He can create the anti-epic.
Mann realizes, however, that that is a very ambiguous act
and may involve the rejection of all the human, moral, and
spiritual values in the inversion of the traditional forms.
Serenus knows what is at stake and is uneasy in his collabora-
tion with Adrian on *Love's Labours' Lost,* "I have always
been rather unhappy at any mockery of humanistic extrava-
gances; it ends by making humanism itself a subject for
mirth." Mann took the risk and created his terrible parody
knowing that he was doing in his art what the Nazis were
doing in the state: saying that the traditional forms had to be
reinterpreted. Since he is creating both Adrian and Serenus,
he can have the courage to do it and to point out to his audience that he is doing it.

Bate has written well of Mann's special sense of the burden
of the past:

> But if we are confronted with the suggestion that one age of
> achievement in the arts may necessarily—because of its great-
> ness, and because of the incorrigible nature of man's mind—
> force a search for difference, even though that difference
> means a retrenchment, we become uneasy. When the change
> in the arts since the Renaissance is attributed to the loss of
> religious faith, to the growth of science, to commercialism, or
> to the development of mass media, we are always at liberty
> to feel that those circumstances may conceivably change
> again. But the deepest fear we have is of the mind of man
> itself, primarily because of its dark unpredictabilities, and
> with them the possibility that the arts could, over the long
> range, be considered as by definition suicidal: that, given
> the massive achievement in the past, they may have no fur-
> ther way to proceed except toward progressive refinement,
> nuance, indirection, and finally, through the continued pres-
> sure for difference, into the various forms of anti-art.
>
> The speculation that this may be so—or that the modern
> spirit is beginning, rightly or wrongly, to believe that it is

so—is a major theme of one of the most disturbing novels of our century, Thomas Mann's *Dr. Faustus*. We find the implications so unsettling, in this modern version of the Faust legend, that we naturally prefer—if we can be brought to linger on the book rather than forget it—to stress other themes, other implications that can be more localized (for instance, the condition of Germany between the two World Wars). For Mann's twentieth-century Faustus, a German composer of genius, all the most fruitful possibilities in music have already been so brilliantly exploited that nothing is now left for the art except a parody of itself and of its past— a self-mockery, technically accomplished but spiritually dead in hope, in short, an "aristocratic nihilism." It is "anti-art" in the sense of art turning finally against itself. And this modern Dr. Faustus, so cerebral and self-conscious before the variety and richness of what has already been done, sells his soul to the devil—as in the old Faust legend—in order to be able once again to produce great art. The special horror is that this involves the willing, the deliberately chosen, destruction of part of his brain in order to free himself from the crippling inhibitions of self-consciousness— a partial destruction of the brain that is to be followed, after the agreed lapse of years, by what he knows beforehand will be a complete disintegration.

Bate is describing Mann's demon, the burden of consciousness with which he endowed Adrian. Joyce and Mann recognize best the seriousness of parody for the modern artist; if the artist cannot escape from the past, he can at least subvert it. If past achievements are to be the measure of one's work, then one can make one's goal the alteration of what was previously done. Mann carries a special additional burden, however, in *Doctor Faustus*: his sense of the German past in the German present in which Serenus writes.

Mann takes as the subject for his parody German music and German philosophy, Germany's greatest contributions to Western civilization. In his novel of the Nazi terror, Mann seems to be saying that the worst in Germany is a parody of

the best. He seems also to be linking the best and the worst
in the German mind in the idea of incest. The Shakespearean
references establish the contrast of the more open, more
hospitable, more polyglot genius of England and America.
It is as if the greatness of German genius had a natural ten-
dency to close back upon itself, to inbreed, and finally become too weak to sustain itself. The Nazi concept of racial
purity for the Aryan is the idea of incest writ large: only the
family is worthy of the family. Adrian says of Germany that
it is "A confused nation . . . and bewildering for the others."
He is answering the pained question of how the Germany of
such genius could become the Germany of such barbarism?
His answer seems to be that the peculiar history of Germany
produced in its greatest minds a sense of isolation which
sought relief by intense and passionate communication with
those to whom they were related in blood. In Mann's special
vision, therefore, greatness is the result of illicit passion and
the denial of human feelings. He makes, therefore, of Adrian
Leverkühn a symbol for the glory and the bestiality of his
country.

The artist is the center of the book, the artist as tyrant and
victim. Mann struggled all his life to represent in his art the
problems of the artist. Only in *Doctor Faustus* did he come
to the realization that the artist and the tyrant must, by their
very nature, take their lives and those of others and turn them
into the instruments of their vision. Having done that, the
artist cannot apologize for himself. He can create his non-
creative counterpart who murmurs, with Serenus, a prayerful
epitaph for the lonely *Mann:* "God be merciful to thy poor
soul, my friend, my Fatherland!"

A Bibliographical Note

I owe a great deal to many scholars and critics. So much, in fact, that I can here acknowledge only my most pressing obligations.

Francis Fergusson, Kenneth Burke, and R. P. Blackmur taught me most of what I know about literature. Their influence is so strong on every page that I can recognize it, but no longer document it.

To Irving Howe's *Politics and the Novel* I have owed so much for so long that I am pleased to give this public thanks to the man who showed a generation how to talk about politics in art.

Chapter One.   The Lamps of Europe

The quotation of Sir Edward Grey is from Barbara Tuchman's book, *The Guns of August.* That work and her other fine study of an era, *The Proud Tower,* influenced very strongly my treatment of the novelists considered.

The maxim of Pound is in the *ABC of Reading.* I read Lewis' in Marshall McLuhan's *Understanding Media.*

The quotation from R. P. Blackmur is from his essay "And Others" in *Form and Value in Modern Poetry*.

Pound's observation on 1870 and the *Education sentimentale*, actually a quotation from Flaubert's letters, is in his essay "Henry James" which I first read in Philip Rahv's collection, *Literature in America*.

The quotation from Kafka is from Gustav Janouch's *Conversations with Kafka*.

Chapter Two.   Hawthorne: The Politics of Puberty

I want to mention here four extraordinary essays in criticism involving Hawthorne's story. Q. D. Leavis' assessment is available in *Hawthorne: A Collection of Critical Essays*, edited by A. N. Kaul. It was this essay, first printed in *The Sewanee Review*, which set me and many others to thinking about the story. The other essays are by Roy Harvey Pearce in *Historicism Once More;* Frederick Crews in *The Sins of the Fathers;* Daniel Hoffman in *Form and Fable in American Fiction*. After a century of neglect, the story has now been well served by its students.

E. M. Forster's famous statement is in *Two Cheers for Democracy*.

The quotation from Lawrence is, as is that in the next chapter, from *Studies in Classic American Literature*.

Chapter Three.   Dostoyevsky: The Political Gospel

I must deal first with two vexing problems, the name of the author and the title of the book. I used Andrew R. MacAndrew's translation in which he, after much thought, selected the traditional *Possessed* over the more current *Devils*. Having decided to use his translation, I thought it logical to use his transcription of "Dostoyevsky" even though my inclination is to omit the first "y." (MacAndrew himself compounds the confusion by using "Dostoevsky" in subsequent translations of that author.)

The biographical data I used derives mostly from E. H. Carr. I also consulted the recent biographies by David Margarshack and Avraham Yarmolinsky. Jessie Coulson's *Dostoyevsky: A Self-Portrait* is a fascinating collection.

I discovered the work of Edward Wasiolek as articles in learned journals when I first faced the problem of teaching Dostoyevsky. For this book I owe a special debt to his edition of *The Notebooks for the Possessed* and to his critical study, *Dostoyevsky: The Major Fiction*.

The quotations from Camus all come from his notes to his adaptation of *The Possessed* for the stage that are printed in the Pléiade edition of his works by Gallimard in Paris, 1962. The translation is mine.

The quotation from Dostoyevsky on himself as a "Nechayevist" is given as it appears in Konstantin Mochulsky's *Dostoyevsky: His Life and Work*, translated by Michael Minihan. The letter to Maikov is also quoted from Mochulsky where Minihan uses *The Devils* as the title of the novel.

Moravia's essay is reprinted in George Gibian's excellent edition of *Crime and Punishment*.

"Steinberg" is A. Steinberg and his *Dostoievsky* is a volume in the Studies in Modern European Literature and Thought series.

George Steiner's *Tolstoy or Dostoyevsky* taught me a good deal about the dramatic structure of *The Possessed*.

In *The Years of the Golden Cockerel* Sidney Harcave reports on the subsequent career of Nechayev. He was arrested in Switzerland in 1872, deported to Russia, tried, and sentenced to life imprisonment. But when the novel was finished, he seemed to be beyond punishment.

Chapter Four.   James: The Aesthetics of Politics

Once upon a time I was a student in a class of Leon Edel's. I think this means that I owe him even a little more than all the other readers of his great biographical study of James.

Oscar Cargill, with whom I disagreed on almost everything, was a fine and thoughtful man. This seems a good place to thank him for the things he taught me in spite of myself.

Alice James' *Diary* has been edited by Leon Edel.

The quotation from Carlyle is from *The French Revolution*.

The quotations from Pound are from "Henry James" in the Rahv collection mentioned in the note to Chapter One. The essay is also in *The Literary Essays* of Ezra Pound, edited by T. S. Eliot. The poetry, of course, is from *Hugh Selwyn Mauberely*.

My debt to Lionel Trilling is obvious. I have learned much from his essay on the novel in *The Liberal Imagination* and from everything else he has written.

Graham Greene's five essays on James in *The Lost Childhood and Other Essays* are not well enough known by readers of James.

Chapter Five.   Conrad: The Price of Politics

The reference to Pound on charged language is to the *ABC of Reading* and *How to Read*.

Hugh Trevor-Roper in his book *Men and Events* set me to thinking about the meaning of European expansion, and it was from him, I think, that I picked up the detail of the conquerors being five feet eight inches tall.

Tawney's and Weber's discussion of the "calling" and the

theology of capitalist expansion are extraordinarily relevant to Conrad's novels.

F. R. Leavis' strictures are from *The Great Tradition,* a book which continues to influence my thinking about fiction.

Robert Penn Warren's essay, the Introduction to the Modern Library *Nostromo,* reprinted in his *Selected Essays,* is as valuable a commentary as one would expect from the author of America's best political novel.

The word "overreacher" and the idea it represents I learned in Harry Levin's study of Christopher Marlowe.

My small quotation from Irving Howe's *Politics and the Novel* in no way indicates what I learned from that serious and humane book.

Chapter Six.   Kafka: The Political Machine

Edwin Berry Burgum is the Marxist critic referred to and I read his essay on Kafka in *The Kafka Problem,* edited by Angel Flores.

The text I used is that in Franz Kafka, *The Complete Stories,* edited by Nahum N. Glatzer, with the translation by Willa and Edwin Muir.

The citations of Heinz Politzer are both to the revised edition of his *Franz Kafka: Parable and Paradox,* the best overall study of Kafka I know.

The references to the diaries and letters are as follows: *Letter to His Father,* translated by Ernest Kaiser and Eithne Wilkins; *Letters to Milena,* edited by Willy Haas and translated by Tania and James Stern; *Diaries, 1910–1913* and *Diaries, 1914–1923,* edited by Max Brod and translated by Joseph Kresh and by Martin Greenberg, with the cooperation of Hannah Arendt.

Speer's *Inside the Third Reich* was published in America in 1970 in a translation by Richard and Clara Winston.

Chapter Seven. Mann: Art, Politics, and the Apocalypse

All quotations of the works are from Helen T. Lowe-Porter's translations for Knopf in *Stories of Three Decades* and *Doctor Faustus*. I also consulted David Luke's more recent translation of "Gladius dei," but used Mrs. Lowe-Porter's for quotation.

The reference to Mann's letters to Felix Bertaux is to Thomas Mann's *Letters,* translated by Richard and Clara Winston.

The comparison of Cipolla to Chaucer's Pardoner I owe to Helaine Newstead and a class lecture to which I came as a casual visitor and stayed as a fascinated listener.

Although they are not cited directly in the text, I found the studies of the novel by Joseph Frank in *The Widening Gyre,* Erich Heller in *The Ironic German,* Roman Karst in *Thomas Mann Oder Der Deutsche Zwiespalt* and, especially, Erich Kahler in *The Orbit of Thomas Mann* very satisfying.

Georg Lukacs is, as a critic of Mann, *sui generis.*

Published in 1951, Henry Hatfield's *Thomas Mann* remains an important study of its subject.

Walter Jackson Bate's book *The Burden of the Past and the English Poet* won the Christian Gauss award in 1971.

Index

187